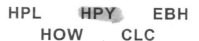

DOLLEY MADISON

Other titles in *Historical American Biographies*

Alexander Graham Bell
Inventor and Teacher
ISBN 0-7660-1096-1

Andrew Carnegie
*Steel King and
Friend to Libraries*
ISBN 0-7660-1212-3

Annie Oakley
Legendary Sharpshooter
ISBN 0-7660-1012-0

Benjamin Franklin
Founding Father and Inventor
ISBN 0-89490-784-0

Buffalo Bill Cody
Western Legend
ISBN 0-7660-1015-5

Clara Barton
Civil War Nurse
ISBN 0-89490-778-6

Dolley Madison
Courageous First Lady
ISBN 0-7660-1092-9

Jeb Stuart
Confederate Cavalry General
ISBN 0-7660-1013-9

Jefferson Davis
President of the Confederacy
ISBN 0-7660-1064-3

Jesse James
Legendary Outlaw
ISBN 0-7660-1055-4

John Wesley Powell
Explorer of the Grand Canyon
ISBN 0-89490-783-2

Lewis and Clark
Explorers of the Northwest
ISBN 0-7660-1016-3

Martha Washington
First Lady
ISBN 0-7660-1017-1

Paul Revere
Rider for the Revolution
ISBN 0-89490-779-4

Robert E. Lee
Southern Hero of the Civil War
ISBN 0-89490-782-4

Stonewall Jackson
Confederate General
ISBN 0-89490-781-6

Susan B. Anthony
*Voice for Women's
Voting Rights*
ISBN 0-89490-780-8

Thomas Alva Edison
Inventor
ISBN 0-7660-1014-7

Historical American Biographies

DOLLEY MADISON

Courageous First Lady

Lynda Pflueger

Enslow Publishers, Inc.

44 Fadem Road   PO Box 38
Box 699   Aldershot
Springfield, NJ 07081   Hants GU12 6BP
USA   UK

Dedication

To Rusty for her loving support.

Library of Congress Cataloging-in-Publication Data

Pflueger, Lynda.
   Dolley Madison : courageous first lady / Lynda Pflueger.
      p.   cm. — (Historical American biographies)
   Includes bibliographical references and index.
   Summary: A biography of the wife of James Madison, focusing on her
role as this country's fourth First Lady.
   ISBN 0-7660-1092-9
   1. Madison, Dolley, 1768–1849—Juvenile literature. 2. Madison,
James, 1751–1836—Juvenile literature. 3. Presidents' spouses—United
States—Biography—Juvenile literature. [1. Madison, Dolley, 1768–1849.
2. First ladies. 3. Women—Biography.]
   I. Title. II. Series.
   E342.1.P48 1999
   973.5'1'092—dc21
   [B]   98-5811
                                                           CIP
                                                            AC

Printed in the United States of America

10 9 8 7 6 5 4 3 2 1

Illustration Credits: Enslow Publishers, Inc., pp. 61, 85; Library of
Congress, pp. 6, 11, 19, 26, 28, 31, 37, 41, 43, 48, 57, 81, 90, 99, 103,
108, 114; Virginia Historical Society, pp. 59, 72.

Cover Illustration: Lynda Pflueger (Background—Montpelier); Library
of Congress (Inset).

CONTENTS

1 The British Are Coming!........ 7

2 Quaker Girl.................. 14

3 The Great Little Madison....... 24

4 Montpelier.................. 40

5 Jefferson's Hostess 50

6 The President's Lady.......... 68

7 War of 1812................. 77

8 Peace 89

9 Later Years................. 94

10 Epilogue.................. 111

Chronology 116

Chapter Notes............... 118

Glossary................... 124

Further Reading............. 126

Index 127

Dolley Madison

1

THE BRITISH ARE COMING!

On June 18, 1812, the United States declared war on England. The British Navy blockaded the American coast and several battles were fought in Canada. Finally, in the summer of 1814, a fleet of British ships landed on the Maryland coast and four thousand soldiers headed for Washington, D.C., the capital of the United States. The British soldiers "swore they would" greet the American president and his wife in their drawing room "and eat their dinner in the Yankee Palace."[1]

On August 23, 1814, President James Madison rode out to Bladensburg, Maryland, to check on the forces that were gathering to protect the capital.

Before he left he urged his wife, Dolley, to go to Virginia, where she would be safe. She refused to go as long as he remained in the capital. As he left, he implored her to take care of herself and make sure his presidential papers were safe.

During the day Dolley Madison received two messages from her husband. The last message asked her to be ready "at a moment's warning to enter [her] carriage and leave the city."[2] Mrs. Madison had placed her husband's papers in trunks and filled her carriage with them, but she was determined not to leave until she knew her husband was safe and could accompany her.

Many times the following morning, the First Lady went upstairs in the President's House and looked out one of the windows through her spy glass, hoping to catch sight of her husband as he returned to the city. Optimistic that the battle would end in an American victory, she ordered her staff to prepare dinner to be served at the usual hour of 3:00 P.M. Paul Jennings, one of the Madisons' servants, later wrote that "I set the table myself, and brought up the ale, cider, and wine, and placed them in the coolers, as all the Cabinet and several military gentlemen and strangers were expected."[3]

At noon Dolley Madison once again looked through her spy glass and was alarmed to see "groups of military wandering in all directions, as if there was a lack of arms, or of spirit to fight for their own firesides [homes]."[4] Three hours later, two messengers arrived covered with dust from their hasty journey and yelling, "Clear out, clear out!"[5] The Battle of Bladensburg had been lost and the American troops were retreating.

The sound of cannon fire could be heard in the distance, but Dolley Madison would not leave. Her staff had acquired a wagon, and she waited until it was filled with her husband's papers, a few books, the household silver, red velvet draperies from one of the parlors, and a small clock. Then, she insisted on waiting until the large portrait of former President George Washington had been removed from the wall and safely taken away. Finally, she got into her coach and sped away on the road leading to Georgetown.

The Burning of Washington

A few hours later, the British entered the city from the opposite direction. Under the command of Rear Admiral Sir George Cockburn and Major General Robert Ross, the British soldiers marched up to the Capitol. The building housed the Hall of Representatives, the Senate Chamber, the Supreme Court Room, and the Congressional Library. The soldiers fired shots through the windows and marched inside. Admiral Cockburn reportedly stood on top of the House speaker's chair and asked, "Shall this harbor of Yankee democracy be

burned?"[6] The soldiers responded positively to the question and the building was set afire.

Then Admiral Cockburn and General Ross ordered their men to march down Pennsylvania Avenue to the President's House. Before they torched the building, they ransacked the house, looking for souvenirs. They found little of value, but did discover a sumptuous dinner set out for forty guests.[7] According to one of the British soldiers,

> Several kinds of wine in handsome cut glass decanters, were cooling on the sideboard; plate holders stood by the fireplace, filled with dishes and plates; knives, forks, and spoons, were arranged for immediate use; in short everything was ready for . . . a ceremonious party.[8]

The soldiers ate the meal and drank President Madison's wines. A few of them expressed their disappointment that the president had escaped, for they had wanted to take him prisoner and "show him in England."[9] Then they set fire to the house. The flames from the burning building lit up the Washington sky and could be seen for thirty miles. During the night a heavy rain turned the fire into smoldering embers. Only the four outside walls of the President's House were left standing.

The next day, the British continued to burn public buildings. They put torches to the War Office and threatened the Patent Office. Dr. William Thornton, the superintendent of the Patent Office, talked them into sparing the building because it

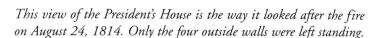

This view of the President's House is the way it looked after the fire on August 24, 1814. Only the four outside walls were left standing.

housed private citizens' inventions. Next, the British soldiers marched to the office of the *National Intelligencer*, a Washington newspaper, and prepared to burn it. Ladies living in the neighborhood, who feared the fire would spread to their homes, talked them out of burning the building.

Admiral Cockburn was still determined to destroy as much as he could of the newspaper because it had criticized him. He ordered his men to demolish the contents of the newspaper's office and to make sure "that all the C's are destroyed" on the newspaper's printing press "so that the rascals can have no further means of abusing my name. . . ."[10]

Admiral Cockburn

Admiral Cockburn rode around the streets of Washington on a white mare, laughing at the terrified women who pleaded with him not to destroy their houses. "Never fear," he said, "you shall be much safer under my administration than Madison's."[11] He was trying to convince the frightened women that they were better off under British rule.

Later that day a hurricane hit Washington, D.C., and stopped the British soldiers from burning more government buildings. George Robert Gleig, a British officer, gave this account of the storm:

> The sky grew suddenly dark, and the most tremendous hurricane . . . came on. Roofs of houses were torn off by it, and whisked into the air like sheets of paper . . . the noise of the wind and thunder, the crash of falling buildings . . . produced the most appalling effect. . . . This lasted for nearly two hours without intermission; during which time, many of the houses spared by us were blown down; and thirty of our men, besides several of the inhabitants, [were] buried beneath their ruins.[12]

When the storm ended, the British retreated. It took four days for them to march back to their ships. They had lost nearly a thousand soldiers who had either been killed in combat, died of fatigue, been taken prisoner, or deserted.[13]

About an hour after the First Lady had left the President's House, James Madison arrived. He was thankful to find that his wife had departed. After resting for a short time, he rode out searching for her. Thirty-six hours later, they were reunited in Virginia.

Four days after leaving Washington, D.C., Dolley Madison returned to the capital and visited the buildings the British had destroyed. Crowds turned out to cheer her. She responded to their cheers "by smiling, waving, and occasionally shaking her fist toward the north, where the British had marched."[14] Later she was praised for her courage and quick action in saving her husband's presidential papers and the priceless painting of George Washington, whom many consider to be the father of our country. She had proven herself to be an extraordinarily brave First Lady.

2

QUAKER GIRL

olley Payne was the third child of John Payne, born on February 9, 1740, and Mary Coles, born on October 14, 1745. Both of her parents were Virginians and grew up in adjoining counties. They were married in 1761. Mary Coles was considered a beauty. She came from a well-established Quaker family. John Payne owned a small farm and was Episcopalian, a member of the Church of England. When Mary married John Payne, the Quakers expelled her for marrying "out of unity."[1] In a short time, she converted her husband to her faith and rejoined the Quaker community.

A year after their marriage, Mary Payne gave birth to their first son, Walter, on November 15, 1762. Four years later, on June 17, 1766, another son, William Temple, was born. Dolley was born on May 20, 1768, in Guilford County, North Carolina. At the time, the Paynes were living in a new Quaker settlement in the wilderness.

When Dolley was nine months old, her family returned to Virginia, where her father bought a large tobacco plantation. The plantation was built by a Scotsman and became known as Scotchtown. The main house was one hundred feet long and nearly fifty feet wide. It consisted of three stories and nineteen rooms. In the main hallway on the first floor was a trapdoor that led to a basement beneath the house.

Dolley's Name

Dolley Madison's early biographers changed the spelling of her first name to Dolly. They also claimed she had been named after her aunt Dorothea Dandridge, the second wife of Patrick Henry, the great American patriot. This is highly unlikely, for Dorothea Dandridge was only eight years old when Dolley was born and she did not marry Patrick Henry until ten years later.

In 1771, when Dolley was three, John Payne sold Scotchtown to Patrick Henry, his wife's cousin, for six hundred pounds. Then, he built a new home nearby on the Coles plantation, where his wife's family lived. The house was probably located on the 176 acres that William Coles gave to his daughter on September 5, 1771. John Payne continued to grow tobacco on his land, and over the next nine years five more children were added to the Payne family: Isaac, Lucy, Anna, Mary, and John.

John and Mary Payne were devout Quakers. After returning from North Carolina to Virginia, they were

Society of Friends

The members of the Society of Friends were also known as Quakers. They came to the American colonies from England to escape religious persecution. George Fox founded the Society of Friends in 1650. An English judge gave Fox the name Quaker when he accused Fox of quaking before God. The basic belief of the Quaker religion is that God dwells in the heart of every person. This is called the Inner Light and is believed to be the voice of God speaking directly to a person's soul. During colonial times, Quakers regarded American Indians as their brothers and strongly opposed slavery. Due to their belief in equality they called everyone "thee" or "thou," which at that time were terms reserved for friends and equals. Also, Quakers were pacifists. They did not believe in war.

appointed clerks of their Quaker community. Since Quakers felt they were the "custodians of the daily lives of their members," clerks were required to document all the important events that occurred in the lives of their members, such as marriages, births, and deaths.[2] In time both Paynes achieved the rank of elders, but only John Payne advanced to the status of minister, or public Friend. This status allowed him to preach.[3]

Dolley attended a Quaker school with her brothers. At that time in Virginia, it was unusual for a girl to attend school. Most families educated only their sons. The schoolhouse the Payne children attended also served as the meetinghouse of the Cedar Creek Quakers. At school Dolley read from the Quaker Book of Discipline and learned to write and do arithmetic.

Dolley was an attractive child with blue eyes and dark hair. She dressed plainly in long, gray muslin dresses that had no tucks, gathers, or buttons. The only extravagance her mother allowed was for her to wear a linen mask over her face to protect her fair skin from the sun.

John and Mary Payne reared their children in the strict discipline of their faith. But Dolley did not always conform to the constraints of her religion. Sometimes she ran races with her brothers and, until she lost it, wore a piece of jewelry secretly hidden under her dress.

Slavery

John and Mary Payne owned eighty slaves, and the issue of slavery weighed heavily on their consciences. Quakers believed that slavery was a sin, but plantations such as theirs could not be profitable without slave labor. In 1769, the members of the Cedar Creek Meeting "unanimously agreed that something be done about it."[4] At the time, it was illegal to free slaves in Virginia.

After the Declaration of Independence was signed in 1776, many Quakers felt the time was right for change. They wrote to Patrick Henry, who was then the Virginia governor. Henry respected Quakers for their "notable efforts to abolish slavery" and spoke out against the deplorable "necessity of holding fellow-men in bondage."[5]

Finally in 1781, the law was changed and John and Mary Payne were among the first Quakers to sacrifice their comfortable lifestyles and free their slaves. They chose Philadelphia, the stronghold for their religion, to be their new home. One of their slaves, Mother Amy, refused to leave the Payne children and went to Philadelphia with the family as a paid servant.

Philadelphia

In 1783, the Paynes arrived in Philadelphia. They moved into a three-story row house. In Philadelphia, houses were built in rows side by side right up against the street. Due to the cramped quarters,

This engraving of the Declaration of Independence with the medallions and seals of the thirteen original colonies shows portraits of John Hancock, George Washington, and Thomas Jefferson.

Dolley and her three sisters shared one of the upstairs bedrooms, and Mother Amy slept in the attic with the younger children. John Payne used the front room downstairs as his office. In 1785, Payne's business was listed in the city directory as a starchmaker at 410 Third Street.

After six years of hard times, John Payne's business went bankrupt. Following common custom, the Quaker community publicly disowned him "for failure to pay his debts."[6] He became an outcast. At the age of forty-nine, he retired to his home and the seclusion of his bedroom. He refused to go out in public again. Mary Payne supported the family by running a boardinghouse in their home.

Her father's misfortune did not seem to affect Dolley's social standing. She was a popular young lady in the Quaker community. When she was eighteen, one of her male cousins described her "as being of slight figure, possessing a delicately oval face, a nose tilted like a flower, jet black hair, and blue eyes of wondrous sweetness."[7]

Dolley Payne had many admirers. When she was twenty-two years old, one admirer, a young Quaker lawyer named John Todd, sought her hand in marriage. At first, she politely refused his proposal, saying that she "never meant to marry."[8] When her father told her he wanted her to marry John Todd, Dolley obediently complied. John Payne had a high opinion of the young lawyer, who had been kind to him despite his financial problems.

As was the Quaker custom, Dolley Payne and John Todd announced their intentions to marry at several Quaker gatherings. Quakers believe that God makes a couple man and wife, so no minister or other official is required to perform a marriage ceremony. On January 7, 1790, John Todd and Dolley Payne stood up at a Quaker meeting and made a mutual and public pledge to each other in which each promised to be a loving and faithful spouse until separated by death.[9] Eighty guests witnessed their pledge and signed their marriage certificate.

After her marriage, Dolley Todd set up housekeeping in a rented house at 85 Chestnut Street. John Todd's law office was located on the first floor, in the front room of the house. His law practice thrived, and in 1792, the couple bought a house of their own.

Early in 1792, Dolley Todd's father, John Payne, died. A simple Quaker funeral was held, with a few of his friends paying final tribute to him. Shortly after his death Mother Amy died, leaving Mary Payne a small inheritance. Over the years, Mother Amy had saved the wages she earned and bequeathed five hundred dollars to her former mistress. The money aided Mrs. Payne in running her boardinghouse. Due to the large number of politicians who frequented the town, which was

then the capital of the United States, her venture proved to be successful.

On February 29, 1792, Dolley Todd gave birth to her first son. He was named John Payne Todd, after her father. She adored her new son, and shortly after his birth, she became pregnant again. The Todds lived quietly within the confines of their religion. The events of the outside world had little effect on them until a yellow fever epidemic raged through the city of Philadelphia in the summer of 1793.

At the time, Thomas Jefferson, the secretary of state, was living in the city. When the epidemic began, Jefferson wrote to a friend, "An infectious and deadly fever has broken out in this place. The deaths . . . during the week before last, were about forty, the last week fifty, and this week I fear they will be two hundred. . . . Everyone is leaving the city who can."[10]

Dolley Todd had recently given birth to her second son, William Temple, when her husband moved the family out of town to a nearby resort called Gray's Ferry on the Schuylkill River. Still weak from childbirth, Dolley Todd was carried on a litter—a device for carrying a sick or injured person. After securing lodgings for his family, John Todd returned to the city. His clients and family needed him, and he spent his time attending to their last requests and preparing their wills. On October 3, 1793, his father, John Todd, Sr., died, and on October 12, his mother passed away.

Finally on October 24, Todd set out to rejoin his family at Gray's Ferry. During the day he became ill and realized he had caught the dreaded fever. When he reached the house where his family was staying, his mother-in-law, Mary Payne, answered the door. "I feel the fever in my veins, but I must see her once more," he told her.[11] Dolley Todd rushed to him. A few hours later he died. Later that day, the Todds' newborn son also died.

Yellow fever ravaged Philadelphia for four months. One of the symptoms of the disease is that its victims turn a yellowish color. The disease was brought to the city aboard a ship from the West Indies and was spread by mosquitoes. During the epidemic, 4,044 Philadelphians died. Dolley Todd and her son Payne, however, survived.

3

THE GREAT LITTLE MADISON

In December 1793, after the yellow fever epidemic had subsided, Dolley Todd returned to Philadelphia with her son, Payne Todd, and her younger sister Anna. Dolley's mother, Mary Payne, went to live with her daughter Lucy. The year before, Lucy had married George Washington's nephew, George Steptoe Washington. The couple lived at Harewood, the family estate in Jefferson County, Virginia. Mrs. Payne, a widow at fifty, had worked hard all her life caring for her family, and now her children decided it was time for them to take care of her.

Young Widow

John Todd left his entire estate to his wife, whom he called "the Dear Wife of my Bosom and the first and only Woman upon whom" all of my "affections were placed."[1] Todd's estate consisted of the house on Chestnut Street and a cash bequest of ten thousand dollars. Although Dolley Todd was not rich, she had enough money to live comfortably. She lived a quiet life with her small family. Her closest friend was Elizabeth Collins, the daughter of a wealthy Quaker merchant who had been a loyal friend to John Payne. Dolley Todd affectionately called Elizabeth Collins "the little mouse."[2] At the age of twenty-five, Dolley Todd was an attractive widow with a full figure, and men "would station themselves where they could see her pass."[3] One of her friends teasingly scolded her for attracting so much attention and remarked, "Really, Dolley, thou must hide thy face, there are so many staring at thee."[4]

One of Dolley Todd's admirers was James Madison, a forty-three-year-old congressman and confirmed bachelor. He asked Senator Aaron Burr, a family friend, to introduce him to the young widow. On hearing that Madison wanted to meet her, Dolley Todd asked Elizabeth Collins for support. She wrote in a note to her friend, "Thou must come to me at once. Burr says that the 'great little Madison' has asked to be brought to see me this evening."[5]

This is Congressman James Madison as he looked around the time he was courting Dolley Payne Todd.

James Madison was a well-known and respected political figure. He had been a delegate to the Continental Congress and helped draft the Articles of Confederation. Later he helped write the United States Constitution and authored the first ten amendments to the Constitution, which are called the Bill of Rights. William Pierce, a Georgia delegate to the Constitutional Convention, once said, concerning the affairs of the United States, Madison had "the most correct knowledge of . . . any man in the Union."[6] Madison also gained the respect of the Quaker community when, as a Virginia legislator, he worked for the "free exercise of religion according to the dictates of conscience."[7]

Dolley Todd met Madison at her home in April 1794. She wore a simple mulberry-colored gown with a matching silk handkerchief and a white cap over her head. Elizabeth Collins, who was engaged to marry Richard Bland Lee, one of Madison's fellow congressmen from Virginia, acted as chaperone.

Their first meeting went well. They reportedly talked about the Philadelphia weather, the poor quality of silk that was currently being imported from France, and gardening. Before Madison left, he invited Dolley Todd and her son to go riding in the country with him.

Madison had fallen in love with Dolley Todd and pursued her hand in marriage. He visited her home several times a week. Before long he was stopping

almost daily with a book for Dolley Todd or a toy for her son, Payne. Madison's attentions did not go unnoticed. Gossip circulated in Philadelphia society about the couple.

In time the gossip reached the presidential mansion and the ear of President George Washington and his wife, Martha. Dolley Todd frequently visited the president's house. She was related to George and Martha Washington through the marriage of her sister, Lucy, to their nephew. On one of Dolley Todd's visits, Martha Washington asked if she were engaged to James Madison. The young widow was startled by the question and said, "'No,' she 'thought not.'"[8]

Martha Washington continued to pursue the subject. "If it is so," she remarked, "do not be ashamed

 to confess it: rather be proud; he will make thee a good husband, and all the better for being so much older. We both approve of it; the esteem and friendship existing between

Martha Washington, the wife of the first president of the United States, encouraged Dolley Todd to marry James Madison.

Mr. Madison and my husband is very great, and we would wish thee to be happy."[9]

Dolley Todd was hesitant to remarry so soon. Her husband had died less than a year ago. She was twenty-six years old, and Madison was forty-three. Also, Madison's career in public life was well established, and he was not a Quaker. She knew her young son needed a father, and she liked Madison, but she needed time to make her decision. Madison asked if she could give him her answer before Congress adjourned in June. Dolley Todd replied that she could not and decided to leave the city for a while to visit her family in Virginia.

With her younger sister Anna and little Payne, she boarded a stagecoach headed for Virginia. In May and June she visited her aunt and uncle in Auburn. During her visit she came down with malaria, an infectious disease transmitted by mosquitoes and characterized by cycles of chills, fever, and sweating.

In August Dolley Todd left her uncle's plantation and headed for Harewood to visit her mother and her sister Lucy. When she left her uncle's home, she was still undecided about Madison's proposal, but in a hotel room near Fredericksburg she made up her mind. From her room she wrote Madison, telling him that she accepted his proposal and would marry him after a proper interval of time. She asked him to meet her at Harewood.

Madison had returned to Montpelier, his family home in Virginia, when Congress adjourned in June. He had written Dolley Todd almost every week, continuing to encourage her to marry him. When he received her letter accepting his proposal, he was delighted. He promptly replied:

> Your precious favor. . . . I cannot express . . . the joy it gave me. . . . I hope you will never have another *deliberation* [thoughtful consideration of both sides of an issue] on that subject. . . . If the sentiments of my heart can guarantee those of yours they assure me . . . there can never be cause for it.[10]

Marriage of Opposites

Within a short time Madison joined Dolley Todd at Harewood. He received a warm welcome from her family. When they were finally alone, he placed on her finger a gold ring adorned with a cluster of eight rose diamonds and urged her to marry him at once. She hesitated. When she married Madison, she would become the sixth member of her family to be disowned by the Society of Friends.

Once again Madison prevailed. Invitations were quickly sent to family members who lived nearby. On September 15, 1794, Reverend Alexander Balmaine married the couple in the stately drawing room of the Harewood house. The groom was elegantly dressed in a short-waisted silk coat and a low-cut vest covered with a cascade of lace ruffles. The lace from his vest was cut into pieces and given to guests as souvenirs.

Whether Dolley Todd abandoned the simplicity of the Quaker style of dress for the wedding is unknown. A great deal was said about what the groom wore, but little about the bride's wedding dress. Madison presented his new wife with a necklace and earrings of carved mosaics representing scenes in Roman history as a wedding gift.

On the morning of her wedding day, the bride wrote to her friend Elizabeth Collins Lee, who was honeymooning in England with her new husband. In her letter she wrote that she had "stolen away" from

This is the room at Harewood in which Dolley and James Madison were married.

her family to tell her friend that on this day she was marrying "the man . . . I most admire . . . and my little Payne will have a generous and kind protector."[11] In her excitement she misdated the letter September 16 instead of September 15. Later that evening she signed the letter, "Dolley Madison! Alas!"[12]

The Madisons honeymooned for a few days in a one-room cottage on the Harewood estate. Five days later they left Harewood, along with Anna and Payne, to visit Nelly Hite, James Madison's sister. The Hites lived in the Shenandoah Valley in Virginia. Mrs. Hite was pregnant and had been unable to make the thirty-mile journey to attend her brother's wedding. Dolley Madison was given a hearty welcome by her in-laws.

For a week, Dolley Madison enjoyed a pleasant visit with her new family. She walked in the gardens, played with Payne and the Hite children, and at times listened to the men talk politics. One of the men's main concerns was England's nasty habit of stopping American ships, stealing their cargoes, and forcing American sailors to join the British Navy. The question of the day was whether the American envoy to England, John Jay, could negotiate a treaty with King George III that would protect the Americans' rights on the high seas.

The couple returned to Harewood, where Dolley Madison suffered a relapse of malaria. In mid-October, they set out for Philadelphia by way of Harpers Ferry. Their route was scenic, but also took them over the most formidable roads. Their new coach was almost shaken to pieces. At one point when the carriage broke down, Madison used his skills to repair the broken parts. By the time the carriage limped into Philadelphia, little Payne was already calling Madison "Papa."[13]

The day after Christmas in 1794, the Quaker community expelled Dolley Madison for having "disregarded the wholesome order of our discipline in the accomplishment of her marriage to a person not in membership with us, before a hireling priest."[14]

She had known the expulsion was coming when she married Madison. Although the Quakers had rejected her, she did not reject them. She still

Early American Roads

In the late eighteenth century, most American roads were made of dirt. In the spring, when snows melted, they turned into mud. In summertime, the roads turned hard and were full of holes. A few roads that were always muddy or steep were covered with logs and then dirt. They were called corduroy roads. Riding on them was like traveling on a giant washboard.

Number of Quakers Decreasing

In the late eighteenth century, many Quakers were marrying outside their religion, which led to their expulsion from the Society of Friends. One observant Philadelphian, Saint-Mery, a French exile who owned a bookstore on First Street, noted in 1790, "the number of Quakers in Philadelphia is decreasing."[15]

considered herself one of them, even though she disliked many of their restrictions. She was not resentful. As far as she was concerned, her fellow Quakers had done their duty. Bolstered by her new husband's love and support, she went on with her life.

The couple lived in Dolley Madison's former home for a short time and then rented a three-story brick house at 115 Spruce Street. They furnished the house with Dolley Madison's furniture, china from Montpelier, and some new purchases from France. It was a happy household. According to family sources, Payne was "as dear to his stepfather as if born to him."[16] Madison also became like a father to his wife's sister, Anna Payne.

Madison's old friend, Thomas Jefferson, worried that since Madison had married, he would retire from public life. While vacationing in Virginia from his duties as secretary of state, Jefferson wrote Madison, wishing him great joy in his married life and cautioning him to, "Hold on, then, my dear friend, that we may not shipwreck. . . . I do not see in the minds of those with whom I converse a greater affliction than the fear of your retirement; but this must not be except to a more splendid . . . and officious post."[17] The post Jefferson was referring to was that of president of the United States. "There I should rejoice to see you," Jefferson added. At the end of his letter, Jefferson asked, "Present me respectfully to Mrs. Madison, and pray her to keep you where you are, for her satisfaction and for the public good."[18]

In January 1795, Dolley Madison learned of the deaths of her brothers William Temple and Isaac. William Temple, a navy ensign, had been living with Isaac in Norfolk, Virginia, when he became ill and died. Shortly afterward, Isaac offended a man, who shot and killed him with a pistol. Dolley Madison was saddened by the deaths and by the disappearance of her brother Walter, who sailed for England in 1785 and was never heard from again.

Philadelphia Society

Dolley Madison found her place in Philadelphia society as if she had been born into it. To please her husband, she began wearing stylish clothes. Ignoring popular fads, she ordered only the styles of dresses, hats, and shoes that suited her. From her mother-in-law, Nelly Madison, she received several pieces of jewelry that had belonged to the family for many

years. Dolley Madison enjoyed the gifts and developed her own, simple style of wearing only one piece of jewelry at a time.

Even James Madison's appearance improved due to his wife's influence. Before his marriage he wore only black, but afterward he appeared in coats of brown, green, and maroon. Madison's attitude regarding social engagements also changed. He was no longer a recluse. With his wife on his arm, he began to enjoy himself.

Political Parties

At the end of George Washington's presidency, two strong political factions developed in the United States. The Federalist party was established in 1787 to promote the establishment of a strong federal government, and its members tended to be pro-British. The party became prominent under the leadership of Alexander Hamilton, the first secretary of the treasury. Hamilton feared the masses and felt the government should be run by aristocratic leaders who knew what was best for the nation.

Thomas Jefferson, along with James Madison, founded the Anti-Federalist party, which later became known as the Democratic-Republican party. They feared a powerful federal government, believed in individual liberty, and wanted to protect the role of state governments. Jefferson believed that if the masses were educated, they could govern themselves.

These oval portraits show George Washington at top and left to right, Thomas Jefferson, James Madison, and John Adams, some of the most influential of the Founding Fathers.

The Madisons entertained often. They invited guests from both political parties, and their home was considered neutral territory. Political discussions were forbidden. Dolley Madison's social skills and her genuine interest in people made her a popular hostess. In 1796, Abigail Adams, wife of John Adams, remarked that "an invitation to dine with Mrs. Madison is prized by all who are asked to her home."[19] Madison was proud of his lovely wife and called her his "beloved." She, in turn, called him her "darling husband" and accompanied him

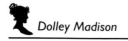

everywhere.[20] She became his confidante and his greatest asset.

When Congress adjourned on March 3, 1796, Madison took his wife home to Montpelier for the first time to meet his parents. During their visit the specifics of John Jay's treaty with England became known. Madison's fears that Jay had been "betrayed by his anxiety to couple us with England, and to avoid returning with his finger in his mouth" came to be a reality.[21] England agreed to evacuate forts in the Northwest, but that was the only concession. There was no mention of the seizing of American ships and the impressment (forcing into service) of American seamen into the British Navy. Tax preferences to American ships were wiped out; American exports such as coffee, sugar, cocoa, molasses, and cotton were prohibited; and the sale of French goods in America was forbidden. Madison was furious. He felt that the treaty was one-sided and Jay had given away too much to the British.

According to the Constitution, treaties had to be approved by a two-thirds vote of the Senate and then signed by the president. On June 24, 1796, the Jay Treaty was approved by the Senate. At first, President Washington refused to sign the treaty. Due to a scandal in his administration—Secretary of State Edmund Randolph was accused of accepting a bribe from the British—Washington changed his mind and signed the document. Ratification of the treaty appeared to be the last straw for Madison. He decided not to run for another term in Congress.

When President Washington announced that he would not seek a third term, the nation's attention focused on the presidential election of 1796. Washington was a Federalist and his party supported Vice President John Adams for president and Thomas Pinckney for vice president. The Democratic-Republican party nominated Thomas Jefferson and Aaron Burr. At that time, the candidate who received the most votes became president and the runner-up, vice president. It did not matter if the men came from different political parties. Thus, John Adams was elected president and Thomas Jefferson, his political opponent, became vice president.

With his friend now elected to the office of vice president, Madison was content to retire and leave the capital to live with his wife at Montpelier. He intended to be a farmer for the rest of his life.

4

MONTPELIER

Dolley and James Madison made their last public appearance in Philadelphia at John Adams's inauguration as president in 1797. The new president, dressed in a neat gray suit, was upstaged by his predecessor, George Washington, who wore his usual black velvet.

One witness to the scene later wrote that the crowd followed Washington as he walked from Congress Hall to the Indian Queen boardinghouse to make his last call on the new president. After Washington stepped inside the inn, "a smothered sound went up from the multitude like thunder, for he was passing away from them to be seen no more."[1] The door of the Indian Queen opened and Washington "stood on the threshold looking at the people. No man ever saw him so deeply moved. The tears rolled down over his cheeks; then he bowed slow and low, and the door closed."[2]

After Adams's inauguration, the Madisons left Philadelphia and went home to Montpelier. Located fifty miles northwest of Richmond, the main house stood on the crest of a hill overlooking the Blue Ridge Mountains. The view from the front of the house was so beautiful it was said to be "within a squirrel's leap of heaven."[3] Madison's parents, James and Nelly, welcomed the couple's return.

Montpelier, James Madison's family estate in Orange, Virginia, became home to Dolley Madison.

They were thankful that their oldest son had come home to give Montpelier his full attention.

Madison took over the operation of a 560-acre section of the plantation, where he grew tobacco, grain, hemp, and red clover. In order to preserve the soil, Madison began working toward rotating the crops every seven years. He also experimented with different types of crops. As time went on, he became more and more fascinated with agriculture and even produced his own fertilizers.

Madison's interest in growing things was shared by his wife. She spent many mornings wearing a big straw hat and working in her garden. Often her mother-in-law would sit outside in the sun and watch her work. Dolley Madison liked to put the seeds in the ground herself, but a small slave boy followed her around, carrying her tools and water. Her garden included tulips, irises, peonies, roses, tiger lilies, nasturtiums, and her favorite flower, oleanders.[4] At times she brought large baskets full of roses into the house. Occasionally, she would pick sprigs of flowers and pin them on the dresses of her young female visitors.

The prosperity of the Madison plantation depended on slave labor. Slavery was an issue that concerned James Madison. As a young man, he so hated the word *slavery* that he could not bring himself to use it, even though his family's livelihood depended on it. James Madison felt "slavery was demoralizing the nations," but he did not believe in emancipation. In his view, freed blacks would be at a great disadvantage in "a white man's society."[5] Madison wanted a national plan established to free the African-American slaves and send them back to Africa.

The Madisons visited their neighbor and close friend, Thomas Jefferson, often. Although Jefferson was vice president, he still spent a great deal of time at home in Virginia. Dolley Madison and Jefferson's oldest daughter, Martha, were about the same age, and they enjoyed each other's company. Patsy, Jefferson's younger daughter, had children near the same age as Payne Todd, and they liked to play together. Laughter often filled the dining room of the house during their visits, but there were also

Monticello, Thomas Jefferson's home near Charlottesville, Virginia, was close enough to Montpelier for the Madisons and Jefferson to maintain a close friendship.

serious conversations. What should they do about the Federalists? What was Hamilton up to now? At other times the conversation turned to farming. Jefferson always listened intently to what Madison had to say on the subject. He considered Madison "the best farmer in the world."[6]

In 1797 James Monroe, another Democratic-Republican, returned from his duties as the United States minister to France and built a home a few miles from Montpelier. The Madisons and Monroes often dined together. Both gentlemen liked to take long walks after dinner, leaving their wives to entertain each other. This must have been difficult for Dolley Madison. She had little in common with Elizabeth Monroe, who was insecure, had no interest in clothes or food, and considered entertaining a chore. Though the two women spent many hours together, they never became close enough to address each other by their first names.

To live more comfortably at Montpelier, Madison enlarged the main house. He added to the existing eight-room house a sixty-foot portico (porch) with white pillars, and thirty feet of additional living space for his new family. He purchased one hundred thousand nails from Jefferson's home-operated factory and one hundred ninety French window-panes from Philadelphia.[7]

When it rained, James and Dolley Madison would take their daily exercise on the new porch.

They determined that they had traveled a mile if they walked back and forth a certain number of times. Occasionally, seven-year-old Payne tagged along behind them. If it rained for any length of time, Madison would run out and pick up the tin measuring cup he left mounted on a fence post in front of the house. By measuring the contents of the cup, he could determine how many inches of rain had watered his fields.

XYZ Affair

Shortly after the Madisons returned to Montpelier from Philadelphia, James Madison received word that war was brewing with France. President Adams had sent a commission of three men to France to work out the differences between the two countries. An attempt was made by members of the French Directory, known only by the letters X, Y, and Z, to bribe the three Americans. Infuriated, the Americans returned home and reported what became known as the XYZ Affair to the public and Congress. To further complicate the situation, France began seizing United States ships. Madison blamed the situation on the Jay Treaty and the United States' lenient policies toward England.

Alien and Sedition Acts

In order to prepare for a possible war with France, the Federalists pushed the Alien and Sedition Acts through Congress. The acts made it difficult

for foreigners to become United States citizens, permitted the president to throw out of the United States any alien he felt was dangerous, and gagged the press to prevent them from criticizing the government. Madison called the passage of the Alien and Sedition Acts "a monster" that "would forever disgrace its parents."[8]

Madison and Jefferson planned to introduce anonymous resolutions against the Alien and Sedition Acts in state legislatures. They felt that the acts went against the Constitution, but the process for defining unconstitutional laws was not yet established. In their resolutions they stated that when the federal government exercised power in areas not specifically delegated to it by the Constitution and established a law, state governments had the right to nullify the law.

Even though Madison planned to stay out of politics, he felt the nation was at stake and he had to fight. In December 1798, he took his wife on a trip to Hanover, Virginia, to ask his cousin, John Taylor, to present his resolution to the Virginia Assembly. Taylor presented the resolution and the day before Christmas, Madison received word that the resolution had passed by a vote of one hundred to sixty-three. Jefferson had a similar resolution introduced and passed in the Kentucky legislature, but other states refused to pass resolutions against the Alien and Sedition Acts.

In the spring of 1799, Madison gave his wife's youngest sister, Mary Payne, away in marriage to Congressman John George Jackson. Twenty-five-year-old Jackson was considered a good catch. Dolley Madison's family came to Montpelier from Harewood for the festivities.

George Washington's Death

Sad news reached Montpelier in December 1799. Unexpectedly, George Washington died at his home, Mount Vernon. Congress declared December 26 an official day of mourning, and many people wore black as if Washington had been a member of their family.

When the news of Washington's death reached them, the Madisons immediately left for Mount Vernon, accompanied by Thomas Jefferson. Dolley Madison, who had always had command of her emotions, cried in public for the first time at Washington's funeral. Her grief was shared by Madison and Jefferson. In a letter to her sister Lucy, Dolley wrote, "We exchanged scarce a word on our sad journey home."[9]

After Washington's funeral, friends started pressuring Madison to return to the Virginia Assembly. The old patriot, Patrick Henry, was running for an assembly seat. He supported the Alien and Sedition Acts. The Democratic-Republicans feared Henry would do everything possible to discredit Madison's Virginia resolution. "Consider that Virginia is the hope of the Republicans throughout the Union," a friend wrote to Madison. "If you will not save yourself or your friends—yet save your country."[10] Madison could not resist his friends' pleas. He reentered political life and ran for the state assembly. The threat Patrick Henry represented was short-lived. On June 6, 1799, the elder statesman died.

This portrait of George Washington, said to be the best likeness of the former president, was painted by Gilbert Stuart.

George Washington's Estate

When George Washington died, he was reported to be one of the richest men in America. His estate was valued at nearly three quarters of a million dollars.[11] Washington stipulated in his will that his slaves would be freed when his wife, Martha Washington, died.

The Federalists and the Democratic-Republicans continued to spar. The nation's future would follow the course set by whichever party won the presidential election of 1800. The Federalists nominated President John Adams and General Charles Cotesworth Pinckney. The Republicans once again nominated Thomas Jefferson and Aaron Burr. As in the election of 1796, the man with the most votes would be president and the runner-up, vice president. The election resulted in a tie, with Jefferson and Burr each receiving seventy-three electoral votes. This threw the decision of who would be president into the House of Representatives. On February 5, balloting began. Six days and thirty-six ballots later, Thomas Jefferson was elected president of the United States. Dolley and James Madison's retirement would soon be over.

JEFFERSON'S HOSTESS

A few months before Jefferson's inauguration, the United States capital was moved from Philadelphia to a new city. Every state in the nation wanted the capital within its territory, so a compromise was made. Before his death, George Washington picked out a tract of undeveloped land in the middle of the United States on the Potomac River. The new city was named after Washington. Instead of becoming part of an existing state, it became a special district called the District of Columbia. The name Columbia was chosen to honor Christopher Columbus, who had discovered America.

Although ten years had already been devoted to building the new capital, the President's House and the Capitol were still not finished. Abigail Adams, the first female occupant of the President's House, had to keep fires burning both day and night to dry out the wet plaster on the walls. She complained that the unfinished East Room was "good for nothing but hanging out wet wash."[1] In the Capitol, carpenters were ordered to stop their hammering whenever Congress was in session.

Outgoing President John Adams did not wait until the end of his term to leave Washington, D.C. He left for his home in Massachusetts in late February. Several of Adams's Cabinet members also left the capital early. They were relieved to be leaving a climate where they froze in the winter and faced unbearable heat in the summer.

Design of the Capitol
A contest was held to determine who would design the Capitol. Some strange entries were received. A bridge builder whose bridges often collapsed sent in an entry. So did a carpenter who liked windowless rooms. The winner of the contest was William Thornton, a Quaker from Philadelphia. Thornton submitted a design that George Washington said combined "grandeur, simplicity, and convenience."[2]

The Jefferson Administration

On the morning of March 4, 1801, Thomas Jefferson, dressed plainly, walked from his boardinghouse to the Capitol. A cannon roared as he entered the north wing of the unfinished building. In the Senate chamber, Supreme Court Chief Justice John Marshall administered the oath of office. Standing next to Jefferson was Vice President Aaron Burr. Jefferson's inaugural address was a conciliatory speech in which he tried to bridge the gap between the two parties. "We are all republicans; we are all federalists," he declared.[3]

The next morning Jefferson announced his Cabinet appointments. No one was surprised to learn that Jefferson had appointed his old friend, James Madison, to the post of secretary of state.

A week after his inauguration, Jefferson left Washington, D.C., to spend a short time at his home, Monticello. He rode on horseback by himself and spent an evening at Montpelier. James Madison had been unable to attend Jefferson's inauguration due to the death of his father and his own poor health. He was confined to bed, suffering from an attack of rheumatism, a chronic illness marked by stiffness and inflammation of the joints.

Jefferson asked the Madisons to come to the capital as soon as possible. He invited them to stay with him at the President's House until they could find other accommodations. Madison promised to take up his new duties as soon as he could, even if he had to be carried to the capital on a stretcher.

On May 1, 1801, the Madisons' carriage jolted down Pennsylvania Avenue, the main road through Washington, D.C., toward the President's House. Accompanying them were nine-year-old Payne and Dolley Madison's sister Anna Payne. The Madisons stayed in the President's House for a short time. Because houses were expensive to buy, they chose to rent a house nearby. The house was small and did not completely meet their needs, but they felt they could manage for a few months. They planned to spend the hot summer months, when Congress was not in session, at Montpelier. When they returned the following fall, they purchased a house of their own on F Street.

The Greatest Cheese in America

To commemorate Jefferson's inauguration, cheese makers in Pennsylvania sent the new president an enormous wheel of cheese. It weighed twelve hundred pounds. Inscribed on it were the words, "The greatest cheese in America for the greatest man in America."[4] It took three weeks and a wagon drawn by six horses to haul the cheese from Pennsylvania to Washington, D.C.

Jefferson's presidential style differed from that of his predecessors. President Washington had conducted business formally, like an English squire. President Adams's administration was also formal, but reflected his New England Puritan background. Jefferson's style, however, was informal and could best be described as simple. He wanted to simplify "the form and ceremony surrounding the President" and give more "consideration to the average man."[5]

The first change Jefferson made was to limit the number of public receptions held at the President's House to two a year, on New Year's Day and on the Fourth of July. He also discontinued the practice of holding weekly receptions to receive guests who wished to see him. Jefferson did not feel they were necessary. He made himself accessible to anyone who wished to see him and greeted everyone with a simple handshake.

Diplomatic Incident

In a short time, Jefferson's lack of formality led to a diplomatic incident. The incident involved the new British ambassador to the United States, Anthony Merry, who arrived in Washington, D.C., in November 1803. After his first meeting with President Jefferson, he complained about having to wait to see him and then about being greeted "in a most undignified manner" by the president in a hallway.[6] The ambassador was shocked by Jefferson's informal dress and the fact that he was wearing carpet slippers. "I could not doubt," wrote the irritated Merry, "that the whole scene was prepared and intended as an insult, not to me personally, perhaps, but to the Sovereign [the king of Great Britain] I represented."[7]

The situation went from bad to worse. Jefferson invited Ambassador Merry and his wife to dinner. They were unaware of the informality of the president's table and assumed the dinner was to be given in Merry's honor.[8] They arrived, expecting to be treated like honored guests. When it was time for dinner to be served, President Jefferson offered his arm to Dolley Madison and escorted her to the table. This was a natural thing for him to do. Since he was a widower, Mrs. Madison often served as his official hostess. After some confusion, James Madison offered his arm to Mrs. Merry and sat next to her at the table. Ambassador Merry headed for a seat near the president, but "A member of the House of Representatives passed quickly by me and took the seat, without Mr. Jefferson's using any means to prevent it."[9]

The ambassador was furious. He sent dispatches to England complaining of his treatment. Mrs. Merry, a tall, well-endowed, and vocal woman, complained about her mistreatment to anyone who would listen. She acquired a small number of influential supporters. The only reprimand she received was at a dinner she attended at the Madisons' home.

She criticized the abundance of food laid out on the dinner table and proclaimed the dinner to be "more like a harvest home supper than the entertainment of a Secretary of State."[10] Dolley Madison tactfully put Mrs. Merry in her place by saying, "The profusion of my table so repugnant to foreign customs arises from the happy circumstances of abundance and prosperity in our country."[11]

Other foreign visitors were also offended by the democratic atmosphere that existed in both the President's House and the home of the secretary of state. Dolley Madison, following the president's example, refused to seat guests according to rank. No one knew who might be seated next to him or her at dinner. At one dinner the French envoy was seated next to a mason who was building a fireplace at his embassy.

Not everyone was offended by the lack of formality. Many members of Washington society were impressed with James Madison's brilliance and Dolley Madison's charming ways. Many newcomers to the city sought Mrs. Madison's aid in getting acquainted, and in a short time she became the "leader of everything fashionable in Washington."[12]

French Fashions

Dolley Madison loved to shop and liked to dress in the most current styles. In 1803, French fashions were the latest rage. The French gowns had low necklines, high waists, and were made of clinging

This portrait of Dolley Madison, Thomas Jefferson's gracious hostess, comes from a painting by Gilbert Stuart.

material. Dolley Madison modified the designs by slightly raising the neckline and using less flimsy materials. By doing so she created gowns that emphasized her best attributes, for she was said to have had "a beautiful neck and lovely shoulders and arms."[13]

Anna Payne

In 1803, Gilbert Stuart, a famous portrait painter, came to Washington for the winter. He painted numerous portraits of politicians and their wives, including James and Dolley Madison. One of his favorite clients was Anna Payne, Dolley Madison's sister. While sitting for Stuart, Anna Payne said it was a shame that he never painted a portrait of himself. In response to her protest, Stuart painted his own profile on the curtain in the background of her portrait.

Anna Payne had grown up to be a lovely young woman with many suitors. Dolley Madison enjoyed

Josephine Bonaparte

Josephine Bonaparte, the wife of the French emperor, Napoleon, was the fashion leader in France. Josephine and her sister-in-law, Pauline, shocked the world by soaking their dresses in water every few hours. The damp dresses clung to their bodies, and the effect was quite startling since they wore no underwear.

When Anna Payne complained that Gilbert Stuart never painted himself, Stuart painted his profile in the background of her portrait.

chaperoning her sister. Shortly after her twenty-first birthday, Anna Payne became engaged to marry Congressman Richard Cutts from Maine. Cutts was a handsome, wealthy lawyer who had been educated both at Harvard University and in France. James Madison liked Cutts, who was also a member of the Democratic-Republican party, and treated him like a son.[14]

On March 20, 1804, Anna Payne married Richard Cutts in the Madisons' drawing room. James Madison gave away the bride and Dolley Madison was the matron of honor. The wedding was covered by the *National Intelligencer*, the Washington newspaper. It reported that the wedding was a "fine affair," and commented, "the presents according to the custom of the time were simply tokens of love, planned and made by those who gave them."[15]

Louisiana Purchase

When France acquired the Louisiana Territory from Spain, President Jefferson sought to buy New Orleans. It was crucial that the United States have the right to freely navigate the Mississippi River and control the port of New Orleans. Roads were poor and the river was the easiest way to transport goods to market. Jefferson never dreamed of acquiring the whole Louisiana Territory, but when French Foreign Minister Charles Maurice Talleyrand asked Jefferson's

President Thomas Jefferson's purchase of the Louisiana Territory from France in 1803 nearly doubled the size of the United States.

representative how much he would pay for all of Louisiana, a deal was quickly made.

On April 30, 1803, the United States paid France $15 million for the 828,000-square-mile area known as Louisiana. This purchase almost doubled the size of the United States. A grand celebration took place at the President's House on July 4, 1803, commemorating the event.

Lewis and Clark Expedition

After the Louisiana Purchase, President Jefferson persuaded Congress to authorize an expedition to explore the new lands and find a route to the Pacific Ocean. Jefferson selected Meriwether Lewis, a quiet man who loved the wilderness and science, and William Clark, a talkative nature lover, to head the expedition together. Jefferson instructed the explorers to establish friendly relationships with the Indians and to make arrangements to begin trading with them.

In May 1804, before Lewis and Clark set out for the unknown regions of the Northwest, Dolley Madison gave a party in honor of the explorers. She, along with the wives of other Cabinet members, gave the explorers simple gifts to make their journey easier. Everyone seemed concerned about their dangerous journey and realized it was unlikely that all the members of the party would return.

Burr and Hamilton Duel

On July 11, 1804, residents of Washington, D.C., were shocked when they heard that Vice President Aaron Burr had killed his rival, Alexander Hamilton, in a duel. Burr blamed Hamilton for his defeat in the presidential race of 1800 and his unsuccessful bid for the governorship of New York. Dolley Madison said little about Burr, who had been a trusted family friend and had introduced her to her husband. Her only documented comment about the incident was in a letter to her sister Anna Cutts, "You have heard, no doubt, of the terrible duel, and death of poor Hamilton."[16]

Philadelphia

Shortly before Jefferson's re-election in 1804, Dolley Madison became ill. She had neglected an injured knee for some time. In June 1805, she wrote to Anna Cutts from her bed, "to which I have been confined for ten days with a bad knee; it has become very painful. . . . I feel as if I should never walk again."[17]

After several weeks of ineffective treatment, James Madison decided to take his wife to the University of Pennsylvania to see the famous surgeon, Dr. Philip Physick.

Madison accompanied his wife to Philadelphia. When they arrived, Dr. Physick put Mrs. Madison's knee in splints and promised that in time she would be cured. From Philadelphia, Dolley Madison wrote to Anna Cutts, "And here I am on my bed with my dear husband sitting anxiously by me, who is my most willing nurse."[18]

Madison stayed with his wife until October, when relations with England and France became unstable and he was needed in Washington. This was the first time since their marriage that the Madisons had been separated for more than a night. In a letter Dolley Madison wrote to her husband shortly after his

departure, she spoke of "the grief . . . I feel at even so short a separation from one who is all to me."[19]

The Madisons corresponded regularly, and a month after James Madison's departure, Dr. Physick released Dolley Madison from his medical care. With great pleasure she wrote her husband, informing him that she would be leaving Philadelphia shortly and was "impatient to be restored" to him.[20]

Return to Washington

With renewed health, Dolley Madison returned to her social life in Washington, D.C. Many interesting visitors converged on the town over the next two years. One of the most colorful was the Tunisian ambassador, Sidi Suliman Mellimelli. The fifty-five-year-old ambassador arrived with a troupe of eleven, including a pipe bearer and three musicians. The Madisons gave a reception for the ambassador. During the affair he caught sight of a female slave who was preparing coffee. The ambassador threw his arms around her and proclaimed that she was the "handsomest woman in America!"[21]

Several representatives from American Indian tribes also came to the capital in the hope of negotiating treaties. Dolley Madison's social register listed ninety-one Indian representatives in all. A few of the Indians wore blue tail coats; some were naked to the waist, their bodies smeared with paint; and others wore hats trimmed in gold or feathers.

Dolley Madison gave several receptions and dinner parties for the Indian delegations. A few of the Indians sat at the dinner table, while others preferred to squat on the floor. With her typical poise, Dolley Madison did not even flinch when she saw an Osage tear off a chunk of meat with his hands and cram it into his mouth. She showed the same courtesy to everyone and made a point of chatting with every guest in her home, whether he was an American Indian or the Tunisian ambassador.

England and France

In 1807, the conflict between England and France escalated. Jefferson extended the United States' policy of neutrality and friendship toward both countries, but maintaining this position became more difficult as each day passed. Both countries were interfering with American shipping, and the British, who were in need of manpower, continued to seize American sailors for their navy. The situation was becoming intolerable.

In June, the *Leopard*, a fifty-gun British frigate, stopped the *Chesapeake*, a thirty-six-gun American frigate, about ten miles outside of Norfolk, Virginia. The British captain accused the American crew of sheltering British deserters. When the Americans refused to turn over the men, the crew of the *Leopard* opened fire. Three Americans were killed and several others injured.[22] The public outcry over

the incident could be heard throughout the country. Many people wanted the United States to retaliate by declaring war on England. Jefferson wrote, "Never since the battle of Lexington [during the American Revolution] have I seen this country in such a state of exasperation."[23]

Jefferson continued to choose the path of peace. He knew that the small United States Navy was no match for the British fleet, and he was convinced the cost of war was too high. Instead, he made provisions to strengthen the armed forces and ban trade with both England and France. The Embargo Act of 1807 was the result of his efforts. The bill was passed by both houses of Congress within four days. It forbade all international trade to and from American ports. The reasoning behind the bill was simple. By confining American ships to their home ports, they could not be confronted by English or French vessels. Both Great Britain and France would be deprived of the American goods they wanted.

The embargo turned out to be an economic disaster. There was no outlet for American exports. Virginia tobacco farmers could not sell their crops, and shipbuilding came to a standstill in New England. Many American merchant ships chose to defy the law and escape from their home ports to trade with the enemy. Congress eventually repealed the Embargo Act.

Jefferson's Successor

At the end of Jefferson's second term as president, it became clear that he intended for James Madison to be his successor. Madison encountered a great deal of opposition. The Federalists wanted a member of their party to be the next president, and several members of the Democratic-Republican party opposed his selection. Madison's critics attacked him both publicly and privately with little justification. During this storm of criticism, James Madison stayed calm and took no offense. He realized that such attacks were part of politics. Through their years of marriage he helped his wife develop the same "impenetrable armor."[24]

THE PRESIDENT'S LADY

James Madison won an overwhelming victory in the presidential election of 1808. He received 122 out of 175 electoral votes. On March 4, 1809, he became the fourth president of the United States. Inauguration day began with a sunrise salute from the cannon at a nearby naval yard. Ten thousand people gathered around the Capitol at noon, and thousands of others lined Pennsylvania Avenue to cheer the new president as he passed. Madison's carriage was escorted by cavalry from Washington, D.C., and nearby Georgetown. Thomas Jefferson was invited to ride with James and Dolley Madison but declined, saying, "the honors of the day belonged to his friend."[1] Jefferson rode to the ceremony on horseback.

The swearing-in ceremony took place in the House of Representatives. Dolley Madison was the first president's wife to witness her husband's inauguration. The oath was administered by Chief Justice John Marshall. After several deafeningly loud cheers, James Madison began his inaugural address.[2] One bystander reported that "Mr. Madison was extremely pale and trembled excessively when he first began to speak, but soon gained confidence and spoke audibly."[3]

An open house was held after the ceremony at the Madisons' home on F Street. Margaret Smith, the wife of the owner of the *National Intelligencer,* described the scene:

> The street was full of carriages and people, and we had to wait near half an hour, before we could get in,—the house was completely filled, parlours, entry, drawing room and bedroom. Near the door of the drawing room Mr. and Mrs. Madison stood to receive their company.[4]

Dolley Madison wore a long white dress with a train made of finely woven cotton. On her head was a bonnet made of purple velvet and white satin with a white feather on top of it. Margaret Smith reported that Dolley Madison "looked like a queen."[5] James Madison wore a suit of wool made from sheep raised in the United States. Handshaking had not yet become the common way of greeting people, and

Madison was almost broken in two by continuously bowing to greet his guests as they proceeded down the receiving line. Dolley Madison served her guests ice cream, bonbons, and Madeira wine.[6]

That evening an inaugural ball was held at Long's Hotel, which later became the site of the Library of Congress.[7] The festivities began when the orchestra played "Mr. Jefferson's March" and the former president entered the room with his secretary. Then, the orchestra played "Mr. Madison's March" and Dolley Madison was escorted into the room by Captain Thomas Tingey, one of the sponsors of the ball. Following his wife, President Madison entered the room, escorting his sister-in-law, Anna Cutts.

Nearly four hundred people crowded into the ball-room, and according to Margaret Smith, Dolley Madison "was almost pressed to death, for everyone crowded round her."[8] She wore a pale buff-colored velvet dress with a long train, and on her head she wore a turban made from the same velvet as her dress and topped with bird-of-paradise feathers.

Though Thomas Jefferson stayed at the ball for only two hours, he was in high spirits. He seemed relieved that the heavy burden of the presidential office had been taken from his shoulders. Also, his affection for Madison was apparent to everyone. While observing Jefferson, Margaret Smith commented that a "father never loved a son more than he loves Mr. Madison."[9]

The President's House

Two weeks after the inauguration, the Madisons moved into the President's House. After eight years of being a bachelor's home, the house had become rundown and shabby. The new First Lady wisely invited influential members of Congress to tour the house. Shortly afterward, Congress appropriated six thousand dollars to refurnish and decorate the interior of the house. Benjamin Latrobe was selected to head the project. A highly respected architect, Latrobe had designed the chambers of the United States Congress and Supreme Court.

Dolley Madison played an important role in the project, and her tastes were reflected in many of the items selected to decorate the house. Her fondness for yellow led to the choice of yellow satin wallpaper for the main drawing room. Ornamental mirrors were hung in many of the rooms to make them look more spacious. She chose patterns for china and silverware and the first permanent musical instruments to be acquired by the mansion, a piano and a guitar.

Shortly after moving into the President's House, Dolley Madison increased the presidential staff from fourteen to thirty. She was fortunate to obtain the services of Jean Pierre Sioussat, who became her head butler and doorkeeper. Sioussat had previously worked for the British ambassador's wife, Mrs. Anthony Merry. The other servants nicknamed him

Dolley Madison loved French fashions and often wore elaborate headdresses and turbans. Guests often complimented her on her stylish wardrobe.

French John because he had been born into a working-class family in the St. Antoine district of Paris, France.

Although Dolley Madison had a house full of servants, she rose early in the morning to do many household chores herself, including her own laundry. While doing her morning chores, she would wear her gray Quaker dress, white apron, and white kerchief.

Wednesday Drawing Rooms

By the end of May, the refurbishing of the President's House had progressed far enough for the First Lady to begin entertaining. She held her first weekly reception on May 31, 1809. The receptions were open houses and became known as Mrs. Madison's crushes or Wednesday drawing rooms. They were of great political importance because they brought together opposing political factions on a regular basis in a cordial atmosphere. Politicians came of their own free will and "decency demanded that rivals behave."[10]

From fifty to two hundred guests would attend the weekly receptions. The affairs began just after sundown and often lasted until nine in the evening. As guests waited to go through Dolley Madison's receiving line, they were serenaded by the soft tones of music played by a military band. Then they enjoyed cookies, cakes, ice cream, and fresh fruit, piled high on buffet tables. The president usually made an appearance sometime during the reception and was often found in the corner of the room, talking privately with another politician.

Washington Irving, a popular author, came to Washington, D.C., hoping to get a political appointment. He wanted the post of secretary to the minister of France. To his disappointment someone else received the job, but still he became a "sworn friend" of Dolley Madison.[11] Irving attended one of

History of Ice Cream

The process of making ice cream gradually developed from the chilling of juices or wines. The Roman emperor, Nero, sent teams of runners into the mountains to bring back snow, which he then flavored with honey, juices, and crushed fruit. Sometime in the sixteenth century, milk was added to these chilled concoctions and a type of sherbet was made.

It is not known exactly when ice cream first appeared in America. In 1700, a guest of Governor William Bladen of Maryland commented about being served ice cream with strawberries and milk for dessert. During the summer of 1790 when the United States capital was in New York City, President George Washington ran up a bill of nearly two hundred dollars with an ice-cream merchant. Ice cream was also a favorite of Thomas Jefferson. Dolley Madison was the first hostess to serve ice cream regularly at state dinners in the President's House.[12]

Mrs. Madison's drawing rooms and gave the following account:

> Here I was most graciously received; found a crowded collection of great and little men, of ugly old women and beautiful young ones, and in ten minutes was hand in glove with half the people in the assemblage. Mrs. Madison is a fine, portly, buxom dame, who has a smile and a pleasant word for everyone . . . but as to Jemmy [James] Madison—Ah! Poor Jemmy!—he is but a withered little apple-John.[13]

Dolley Madison's young cousin, William Preston, attended one of her receptions and noted that she entered the room with a book in her hand. "Still you have time to read?" he asked her.[14] "Oh, no," she said, "not a word: I have this book in my hand—a very fine copy of Don Quixote—to have something not ungraceful to say, and if need be to supply a word of talk."[15]

At another reception, Dolley Madison noticed a young gentleman who seemed ill at ease. When she walked over to him, he was so startled by her attention that he spilled his drink. Then he dropped his saucer on the floor and stuffed his cup into his pants pocket. Mrs. Madison ignored his odd behavior and tried to calm her embarrassed guest by commenting that in such a crowded room "no one could avoid a mishap."[16] Then she asked a servant to bring him another cup of coffee.

The Madisons also gave frequent dinner parties. At these affairs Dolley Madison always sat at the head of the table, President Madison on the side,

and the president's secretary, Edward Coles, at the end of the table. This relieved the president from serving his guests. It also spared him from having to lead conversations, a task he was not good at but at which his wife excelled.

First Wedding in the President's House

During the winter and spring of 1812, Dolley Madison's widowed sister, Lucy Payne Washington, came to visit. Lucy was a beautiful woman in her mid-thirties. In a short time she became one of Washington, D.C.'s most popular ladies and had many suitors. One of her most ardent admirers was Justice Thomas Todd of Kentucky, a member of the Supreme Court. When he proposed, Lucy declined. Todd was a widower with five children, and she already had three boys. Plus, his home was in Kentucky, which she felt was too far away.

Discouraged, Todd left Washington, D.C., when the Supreme Court adjourned and headed home to Kentucky. He had just left when Lucy began to fret about her decision. Finally, she changed her mind and sent a messenger to hurry after him. The messenger caught up to him in Lancaster, Pennsylvania, a three- to four-day journey from Washington. Delighted with the news, Todd turned around and headed back to Washington and his future bride. On March 29, 1812, Lucy and Todd were married. This was the first time a member of a president's family was married in the President's House.

7

WAR OF 1812

In 1811, war clouds hung over the American horizon. On December 22, Dolley Madison wrote her sister Anna Cutts, telling her that a ship had been sent to England, carrying dispatches informing the British that the United States was determined to fight for its rights. She added that "she believed there would be war."[1]

Many United States citizens had tired of playing games with Great Britain and France and were demanding war. The powerful British Navy continued to seize American ships, confiscating their cargoes and impressing American sailors. France, although claiming to respect America's neutrality at sea, had confiscated $10 million worth of property from American ships.[2]

In the fall of 1811, a group of thirty war-hungry young men was elected to Congress. They became known as War Hawks and were led by Henry Clay of Kentucky, who became the speaker of the House of Representatives, and Congressman John C. Calhoun of South Carolina. The War Hawks wanted to restore the honor of their nation and demanded a declaration of war. At first, James Madison tried to block Congress from declaring war. He imposed another embargo, but in time he accepted the fact that war was inevitable.

On June 18, 1812, the *National Intelligencer* announced the United States' declaration of war on Great Britain. Two days later, the news of war reached New York, where several merchant ships sat idle in the harbor. The ships were inactive due to the embargo. Over the tops of the ships' masts hung tar barrels, which had been placed there to protect the wood masts from rotting. They were known as "Madison's night-caps" because they resembled the caps that some people wore on their heads at night to keep warm.[3] Next to the merchant ships were four American warships: the *President*, the *Congress*, the *Hornet*, and the *Argus*. On Sunday, June 21, the four ships left New York Harbor and put to sea, looking for British warships. The second war with England had begun.

After launching warships, the United States initiated a land campaign against Great Britain in Canada. The American plan consisted of a three-point invasion of Canada: along the Great Lakes at Detroit, on the Niagara River, and at the foot of Lake Champlain. In July 1812, an American force of about two thousand men under the command of General William Hull left Detroit and began the invasion of Canada. Hull appealed to the Canadians to join him in putting down the "tyranny and oppression" of Great Britain and to receive "the blessings of American liberty."[4] The Canadians ignored his plea. When Hull received false reports that his troops were greatly outnumbered, he hurriedly fell back to United States territory. On August 16, he surrendered to a small force of English soldiers without firing a shot.

Land Battles

On October 10, a small force of volunteer militia from New York and a few United States Army regulars commanded by General Stephen Van Rensselaer crossed the Niagara River to attack the British at Queenston. The first group of soldiers to cross the river was shot down. The remaining American soldiers refused to cross the border into Canada. They had heard a false rumor that if a volunteer crossed onto foreign soil, he automatically became a regular in the United States Army and was liable for five years of military service.

The following month, Major General Henry Dearborn, a senior officer in the United States Army, sent a force from Plattsburgh, New York, on Lake Champlain, across the Canadian border. When the soldiers refused to advance any farther, Dearborn was forced to return to his winter quarters at Plattsburgh.

Victories at Sea

The war on land did not go well for the Americans, but the small American Navy faired better. On August 19, the United States warship *Constitution* destroyed the British vessel *Guerriere*. It was a great victory, for the *Guerriere* had previously seized many United States seamen. On October 18, the United States sloop *Wasp* captured the British frigate *Frolic*. Later in the month, on October 25, an American warship named *United States* defeated the British frigate *Macedonian*.

The American naval victories were celebrated in Washington with a grand naval ball at Tomlinson's Hotel in November. During the ball, Lieutenant Hamilton, a member of the crew of the warship *United States* and son of Paul Hamilton, the secretary of war, entered carrying the flag of the British frigate *Macedonian*. Four naval officers, each holding one of the four corners of the flag, paraded around the dance floor while the band played "Yankee Doodle." Then, Lieutenant Hamilton laid the flag at Dolley Madison's feet.

This painting shows the victory of the frigate United States *over the British ship* Macedonian.

A woman in the audience described Dolley Madison's reaction to the honor. "Mrs. Madison is said to [use] rouge . . . I do not think it true, as I am well assured I saw her color come and go at the naval ball, when the Macedonian flag was presented to her by young Hamilton."[5]

Election of 1812

In the fall of 1812, James Madison ran for re-election. The Federalists called the War of 1812 "Mr. Madison's War" and worked hard to defeat him. So did a few members of his own political party.[6] Despite their efforts, Madison was reelected.

Prior to the election, Dolley Madison continued to welcome members of both political parties to her weekly drawing rooms. It was commonly believed that these affairs, where people socialized and could speak freely to each other, helped promote political tolerance during troubled times.[7]

Although there were many American naval victories, the British maintained their superiority at sea until September 1813 when twenty-eight-year-old Captain Oliver Hazard Perry defeated the British fleet in the Battle of Lake Erie. This forced the British to pull out of Detroit and cross the border back into Canada. Accompanying the British forces were six hundred Indians led by Chief Tecumseh. American General William H. Harrison pursued the British with a force of three thousand men. When both armies reached Moraviantown, on the Thames

River in Ontario, the Battle of Thames River took place. After the first round of fire, many of the British soldiers fled. During the battle, Tecumseh was killed. This ended England's alliance with the American Indian tribes that had supported them.

War Ends in Europe

In 1814, after Great Britain's war with France ended in Europe, Great Britain sent a large contingent of experienced soldiers to America. After burning government buildings in Washington, D.C., and being forced out of the city by a hurricane, the British soldiers advanced to nearby Alexandria, Virginia.

Fearing that the British would demolish their city, the people of Alexandria surrendered and

Thomas Jefferson's Library

After the British burned the Capitol, Thomas Jefferson wrote to Congress, offering his personal library of nearly ten thousand books to replace the Congressional Library that had been destroyed in the fire. Congress decided to purchase Jefferson's library for $23,900. Jefferson and his granddaughters sorted his books and supervised their packing. It took ten wagons a week to transport the books from Monticello over Virginia roads to the capital. Jefferson's books became the foundation for the current Library of Congress.

offered provisions to the British troops as ransom to save their city. From Alexandria the British marched to Baltimore, Maryland. The British soldiers hated Baltimore, for it was the home of the private sailing ships that had been capturing and sinking British vessels. The British planned to show the town no mercy.

Unlike Washington, D.C., where few preparations were made for the British attack, the citizens of Baltimore were ready. Under the leadership of Major Samuel Smith, merchant ships were sunk in the harbor to create a barrier, trenches were dug, cannons were placed, and local militias were drilled in preparation for the attack. A letter printed in the Baltimore newspaper, the *Evening Post*, stated, "White and black are all at work together. You'll see master and his slave digging side by side. There is no distinction, whatsoever."[8]

Fort McHenry was the major military facility that protected Baltimore Harbor. The commander of the fort, Major George Armistead, ordered his men to fly a giant American flag "so that the British will have no difficulty seeing it at a distance."[9]

Shortly after the British fleet entered Baltimore Harbor, it was approached by a small ship flying a flag of truce. On the ship was Francis Scott Key, a Washington lawyer who had fought in the Battle of Bladensburg. He had been sent by President Madison to rescue William Beannes, an elderly

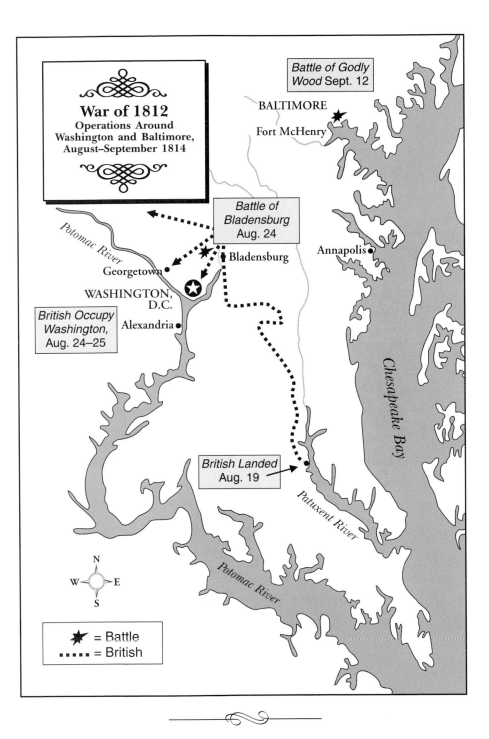

Giant Flag

Well-known Baltimore flagmaker Mary Pickersgill and her thirteen-year-old daughter, Caroline, made the giant flag flown at Fort McHenry out of red and white strips of English wool. Then they added a square piece of blue wool bearing fifteen white cotton stars that each measured two feet across. When completed, the flag was forty-two feet by thirty feet.

doctor who had been taken prisoner by Admiral Cockburn's squadron for interfering with British troop movements. At first, Cockburn refused to release Beannes. When Key showed him letters from British prisoners of war stating that they were being treated well, he relented. However, the truce ship was not allowed to return to the American side until after the battle.

The bombardment of Fort McHenry began at seven in the morning on September 13, 1814, and lasted for twenty-five hours. Key and Beannes witnessed the battle, and throughout the night they watched the "rocket's red glare" and listened to "bombs bursting in air."[10] Near dawn on the morning of September 14, it grew quiet and Beannes asked Key, "Is the flag still there?"[11] Key replied, "Yes, it is still there!"[12] Key was inspired by what he saw and

Beannes's question. On the back of an envelope, he wrote a poem that later became "The Star-Spangled Banner," the national anthem of the United States.

The British fired more than fifteen hundred shells during the battle but were not able to gain access to Baltimore Harbor. When their commander, General Robert Ross, was killed, they retreated and the Americans won the battle. Only four Americans were killed and twenty-four wounded.

Treaty of Ghent

Czar Alexander I of Russia offered to mediate between the United States and Great Britain. Since Russia was the only nation in Europe respected by both England and France, President Madison decided to accept the czar's offer. He sent a special commission, led by John Quincy Adams, to Europe. The other members of the commission were Senator James A. Bayard and Secretary of the Treasury Albert Gallatin. Payne Todd, the president's stepson, also joined the delegation as an aide.

In the small Flemish town of Ghent on December 24, 1814, the American commissioners signed a peace treaty with Great Britain. Unfortunately, word of the treaty did not reach Washington until the last battle of the war was fought in New Orleans on January 18, 1815. The British intended to capture New Orleans, but the French smuggler, Jean Laffite, informed American General Andrew Jackson of their plans. When the eight thousand

British troops landed in New Orleans, Jackson's five thousand men defeated them. The British lost nearly two thousand men, while Jackson's forces lost only seventy-one. The British retreated and headed home.

The war was finally over, and once again the Americans had defeated the British and secured their independence.

8

PEACE

In February 1815, word reached Washington, D.C., that a peace treaty had been negotiated, and "The city now went wild with joy."[1] The Madisons were temporarily living in the Octagon House, the most elegant private home in the city. The house had been built by John Tayloe, a wealthy Virginian, and was leased to the Madisons after the British burned the President's House. Paul Jennings, one of the Madisons' servants, later wrote that Sally Coles, Dolley Madison's cousin, came to the head of the stairs leading to the basement and cried out, "Peace! Peace!"[2] Then she told the butler to serve

The Octagon House, where the Madisons lived for a while after the burning of the President's House, was named for its peculiar shape.

wine to all the servants. Paul Jennings picked up his violin and played the "President's March."

Upstairs in the Madisons' drawing room, a large crowd gathered to celebrate the news of peace. While his guests were enjoying the wine, the president and his advisors went upstairs to look over the treaty, which was called the Treaty of Ghent. They discovered that the document did not address the causes of the war, nor had the British made any concessions. However, the president, wanting to end the war, decided to sign the treaty anyway. The next day, the Senate approved it. A few weeks later, in a letter to Thomas Jefferson, James Madison called the "affair at New Orleans" a better guarantee of peace than the Treaty of Ghent.[3]

A New Home

The Madisons spent the summer of 1815 at Montpelier. When they returned to Washington, D.C., they moved out of the Octagon House and into a smaller house on the corner of Pennsylvania Avenue and Nineteenth Street. There was no front yard, and as people passed by they could look into the windows on the first floor.

Dolley Madison's pet parrot, Polly, sat in her cage in front of one of the downstairs windows. Schoolchildren liked to stand in front of the window and watch Dolley Madison feed her colorful pet. While feeding the bird she would put on a little show and have the parrot talk for the children. One man recalled that Dolley Madison "as well as her pet were very engaging. I can clearly recall her as she appeared in her inevitable turban."[4]

In the fall of 1815, soldiers who had fought in the War of 1812 were being discharged from the army. As they headed for home, their companies would march down Pennsylvania Avenue and pause at the corner of Nineteenth Street, where they gave three cheers for Dolley Madison. Then, they waited for her to come out on the front steps of the house to wish them "Godspeed" in returning home.[5]

Payne Todd finally returned from Europe in the fall. His six-month stay had stretched into two years. Because President Madison was his stepfather, Todd had been treated like a prince by European society. Henry Clay once reminded Todd how he and the other peace commissioners "sat in a gallery and watched you dance with the Czar's sister. . . ."[6] The privilege of dancing with royalty was not extended to the peace commissioners, because they were not considered to be of royal blood. During his travels, Payne Todd learned to speak a little French, acquired a great deal of artwork, and ran up a debt of sixty-five hundred dollars, which his stepfather had to repay.

Despite the disadvantages of entertaining in a smaller and less elegant home, Dolley Madison continued her weekly receptions. In February 1816, she

Easter Egg Hunt

In Europe, Payne Todd learned about the early Egyptian practice of holding an egg hunt or roll. He shared this idea with his mother. Dolley Madison thought an egg hunt would be a delightful party game for children. With her own hands she dyed hundreds of hard-boiled eggs and invited the children in her neighborhood to come and play with them. This event later turned into the White House Easter Egg Hunt that is still held every year.

gave what was said to be "the most splendid Presidential Reception ever given to that date" for the special ambassador from Great Britain, Sir Charles Bagot.[7] To compensate for the dim lighting in the Madisons' drawing room, servants holding lighted candles or torches stood in front of the windows. The house was so brilliantly illuminated that many people remembered it as the "house of a thousand candles."[8]

Dolley Madison wore a rose-colored gown with a long white velvet train. The train was lined with lavender satin and edged with lace. On her head she wore a white velvet turban adorned with golden thread and the tips of ostrich feathers. That evening Sir Bagot, who was well acquainted with the ladies from the royal courts of Europe, declared that the First Lady was "every inch a queen."[9]

Along with entertaining, Dolley Madison also found time to help establish an orphanage in Washington for children whose parents had died during the War of 1812. She was elected the first directress of the organization and donated twenty dollars and a cow. She spent a great deal of time during the winter months cutting out and sewing children's clothes. When she was asked about her sore, blistered fingers, she replied, "Oh, it was delicious work; I never enjoyed anything as much."[10]

9

LATER YEARS

In the fall of 1816, James Monroe was elected president of the United States. On May 4, 1817, the Madisons attended his inauguration. Monroe was the first president to be inaugurated in an outdoor ceremony, due to a quarrel between the Senate and the House of Representatives, both of which had wanted the inauguration to be held in their chambers. After the ceremonies, the Madisons left Washington by steamboat and headed home to Montpelier.

James K. Paulding, secretary of the Navy Board, accompanied them on the boat and later wrote that if ever a "man sincerely rejoiced in being freed from the cares of public life," it appeared to be Madison.[1] According to Paulding, "During the voyage he was as playful as a child; talked and joked with everybody on board, and reminded me of a schoolboy on a long vacation."[2]

Montpelier

Once again the Madisons settled down to life as country farmers. They spent their time running their estate, preparing Madison's notes from the Constitutional Convention for publication, and entertaining a seemingly endless stream of guests. Distinguished foreign visitors, old political friends, family members, and even strangers journeyed to Montpelier. Whoever knocked on the door was welcomed.

At times there were nearly a hundred guests for dinner. In 1820, Dolley Madison wrote to her sister Anna Cutts that on July 4, "we had ninety persons dine with us at one table—put up on the lawn, under a thick arbor."[3] Then she added that only a dozen of the guests stayed all night and that she was "less worried" about having "a hundred visitors" at Montpelier than entertaining twenty-five when she lived in Washington, D.C.[4]

Dolley Madison particularly enjoyed the visits of young people. When she was sixty years old, Samuel Harrison Smith and his wife, Margaret, came to visit Montpelier with their daughter Anna Maria. Dolley

Madison called Anna Maria "my little girl," and one day when they were on the portico, she took Anna Maria by the hand and said, "come let us run a race. I do not believe you can out run me. Madison and I often run races here when the weather does not allow us to walk."[5] Margaret Smith later wrote that despite her age, Dolley Madison ran very briskly, which was more than Smith said she could have done at the time.

While the Smiths were visiting, Dolley Madison took Margaret Smith to meet her mother-in-law, Nelly Madison, who lived in the right wing of the Montpelier mansion. The older Mrs. Madison was ninety-seven years old. When they entered her quarters, she was reclining on a couch, knitting. Mrs. Smith asked how she was feeling. The elder Mrs. Madison replied, "I have been a blest woman . . . I have no sickness, no pain; excepting my hearing, my senses are but little impaired. I pass my time reading and knitting."[6] They talked about the infirmities of old age and Mrs. Madison looked at her daughter-in-law and said, "She is my mother now, and tenderly cares for all my wants."[7] Nelly Madison died shortly after the Smiths' visit and was buried in the family cemetery at Montpelier.

A few years later in August 1832, Dolley Madison received the sad news that her beloved "sister-child," Anna Payne Cutts, had died suddenly.[8] Anna Cutts was eleven years younger than Dolley Madison, and for fourteen years prior to Cutts's marriage, the two sisters had been inseparable. After her sister's death, Dolley Madison remained close to Anna Cutts's seven children.

In 1830, the Madisons received word from a family friend, Anthony Morris, that Payne Todd was in debtors' prison in Philadelphia. Todd owed six hundred dollars and, according to Morris, was very anxious to return home to Montpelier. Once again James Madison paid his stepson's debt. Over the years he spent approximately forty thousand dollars rescuing Todd. Many times Madison paid Payne Todd's debts quietly in an attempt to prevent his wife from worrying about her son.

In the spring of 1835, the famous English writer, Harriet Martineau, visited the Madisons. When she arrived, she was warmly greeted by Dolley Madison and then taken to James Madison's chambers. Martineau later wrote that Madison

> suffered so severely from rheumatism, that during the winter he confined himself to one room; rising after breakfast before nine o'clock, and sitting in his easy-chair till ten at night. . . . He appeared perfectly well during my visit, and was a wonderful man of eighty-three. He complained of one ear being deaf, and that his sight, which had never been perfect, prevented his reading . . . but he could hear Mrs. Madison read, and I did not perceive that he lost any part of the conversation . . .[9]

Martineau also wrote that Dolley Madison was "a strong-minded woman fully capable of entering into her husband's occupations and cares, and there is little doubt that he owed much to her intellectual companionship."[10]

James Madison's Death

As James Madison became more crippled with rheumatism, he was confined to his bed, with his wife as his devoted nurse. Their niece, Mary Cutts, wrote in her memoirs that her aunt would not leave her uncle "for more than half an hour" and that "he was her sole thought."[11]

As her husband grew weaker, Dolley Madison could not conceal her sadness. The thought of losing her companion of thirty-nine years brought her to tears. Madison begged her "to be composed if not cheerful."[12] He did not want his illness to spoil their remaining time together.

Paul Jennings, Madison's slave and servant, wrote that for six months before his death, Madison "was unable to walk, and spent most of his time reclined on a couch; but his mind was bright, and with his numerous visitors he talked with as much animation and strength of voice as I ever heard him in his best days."[13]

Ten years earlier, Thomas Jefferson, Madison's dearest friend, had died on July 4, the date that commemorated the nation's independence from England. In June 1836, Madison's doctors wanted to

This portrait of James Madison was done when he was eighty-two, after his retirement from politics.

give him drugs that would help prolong his life until July 4, but Madison declined. He died on the morning of June 28. Dolley Madison had stepped away from her husband's bedside when his breakfast tray was brought to him. He began to eat, but seemed to be having trouble swallowing. His niece, Nelly Willis, was sitting with him and asked, "What is the matter, Uncle James?"[14] Madison replied, "Nothing more than a change of *mind*, my dear."[15] Then his head dropped, he stopped breathing, and he died.

Three days later, Madison was buried in the Montpelier family cemetery, half a mile south of the house. His black walnut coffin made from Montpelier trees was carried to the cemetery by neighbors. A large procession of family, friends, and slaves followed the casket. After the graveside service, as Madison's coffin was lowered into the ground, "a great inconsolable cry" escaped the lips of Madison's one hundred slaves.[16]

In his will Madison left his entire library to the University of Virginia and bequeathed nine thousand dollars to set up an educational fund for his nieces and nephews. The remainder of his estate, including Montpelier, a house in Washington, and his notes on the Constitutional Convention, were left to his wife. He did not free his slaves because he felt doing so would leave his wife to a life of poverty.

For a year after her husband's death, Dolley Madison remained at Montpelier, surrounded by family members. Her brother, John Payne, postponed his move to Kentucky in order to help his sister organize her husband's papers. When her brother was finally ready to depart, Dolley Madison convinced him to let his third daughter, Anna, stay and live with her as a daughter. Anna was a young woman with "a strong sense of duty," and she became her aunt's constant companion.[17]

Following her husband's instructions and in hopes of meeting her immediate financial needs, Dolley Madison tried to find a publisher for the notes James Madison had taken during the Constitutional Convention. The notes, when published, filled nearly six hundred pages and were divided into three volumes. In the fall of 1836, when she had not been able to find a reputable publisher, she brought the matter to President Andrew Jackson's attention. Four months later Congress, in a joint resolution signed by both houses, appropriated thirty thousand dollars to purchase Madison's notes.

There were several more volumes of Madison's papers that he had hoped to have published. Immediately after selling the first three volumes, Dolley Madison began preparing the remaining papers for publication. It was an exhausting task, and she soon became ill due to fatigue. Her eyesight

became so bad that she no longer could read and had to be assisted in writing letters. She trained her niece, Anna, to imitate her handwriting. Dolley Madison would write the beginning of the letter and the closing words, but Anna would write the main body of the correspondence as her aunt dictated to her.

Dolley Madison Returns to Washington

After Dolley Madison recovered, she decided to return to Washington, D.C. She moved into the small house her husband had left her on Lafayette Square near the President's House. Mary Cutts, the daughter of Dolley's beloved sister Anna, witnessed her aunt's return and wrote in her memoirs that her aunt was warmly received "by those who had formerly known her and those who desired to know this 'First Lady of the Land.'"[18] Dolley Madison had been away for twenty years, but within a short time she once again became the "toast of Washington Society."[19]

Within a few years, the money Dolley Madison had received from Congress for the sale of her husband's papers had been spent. To add to her financial distress, crops had failed and Montpelier was not producing enough to pay for its own operations. In the summer of 1839, she returned to Montpelier with her sister Lucy for a year and tried to run the plantation herself. Due to a difficult economy and a troublesome overseer, she was

This is the house in Washington, D.C., where Dolley Madison lived for the last twelve years of her life.

unable to turn the plantation around and once again, returned to Washington.

Payne Todd continued to run up huge gambling debts, drink to excess, and mismanage the Madison property. Even so, he tried to help his mother by borrowing money from brokers at a high rate of interest. Although the loans brought temporary relief, in the long run they made matters worse when the time came to repay them. Finally in 1842, Dolley Madison decided to go to New York City to visit an old friend, John Jacob Astor. He was one of the wealthiest men in the United States, and she hoped to obtain a loan from him. Using her house in Washington as security, Astor loaned her four thousand dollars.

At the time, Dolley Madison was confident she would be able to sell her husband's remaining papers

John Jacob Astor

Born in Germany in 1763, Astor came to the United States in 1783. Shortly after his arrival, he entered the fur-trading business. By 1800, he had acquired a small fortune and established the American Fur Company. In later years, Astor invested the profits from his fur-trading business in Manhattan Island farmland, which became the heart of New York City. When Astor died, his estate was estimated to be worth more than $20 million.

by the time the loan was due. Unfortunately, this did not happen, and in a few years her financial situation became even more distressing. On July 5, 1844, she received a letter from her servants at Montpelier that said:

My Mistress:

I don't like to send you bad news but the condition of all of us your servants is very bad, and we do not know whether you are acquainted with it. The sheriff has taken all of us and says he will sell us at the next court unless something is done before to prevent it. We are afraid that we will be bought . . . and sent away from our husbands and wives. . . . The sale is only a fortnight from next Monday but perhaps you could make some bargain with somebody by which we could be kept together.[20]

(—Sarah, on behalf of all the servants)

Dolley Madison had no options. Her only choice was to sell Montpelier to someone who would take care of her former servants. Within a month, she made arrangements for the sale. Henry W. Moncure, who had previously bought a small portion of the estate, purchased the rest of the plantation for eighteen dollars per acre, a price well below market value. Dolley Madison retained ownership of a few slaves, some of the furniture from the house, and the family burial plot.

One of the servants Dolley Madison retained was Paul Jennings. He had faithfully served the Madisons for nearly thirty years. Daniel Webster, the famous orator and Madison's neighbor in Washington, bought Jennings from her for $120 on the understanding that Jennings would be able to work to buy his own freedom. Jennings later wrote that Webster often sent him to Dolley Madison's house "with a market-basket full of provisions, and told me whenever I saw anything in the house that I thought she was in need of, to take it to her. I often did this, and occasionally gave her small sums from my own pocket. . . ."[21]

Dolley Madison continued to pursue publication of her husband's remaining papers, but Congress dragged its feet concerning the sale. On January 8, 1844, however, the House of Representatives did pay her an unusual honor. It voted her an honorary seat in its hall. This meant that there would always be a seat for her when she came to watch the proceedings. At the time, this was the highest compliment ever paid to a woman in the United States.

In 1844, Dolley Madison was paid another honor. She was present in the Capitol when Samuel F. B. Morse sent the first telegraph message transmitted between two cities, Washington, D.C., and Baltimore. First, Morse received a four-word message from Baltimore, dictated by Annie Ellsworth, which said, "What hath God wrought."[22] Then, Morse turned to Dolley Madison and asked if she would like to send a telegram to Baltimore. She remembered that one of her cousins lived in Baltimore and dictated, "Message from Mrs. Madison. She sends her love to Mrs. Wethered."[23]

In her later years, Dolley Madison tried to cleverly hide her age. When a friend asked her how old she was, she replied that she was seventy-two. The following year, her friend asked her again and again she replied "seventy-two." Still another year later, her friend asked one more time, and once again Dolley Madison replied "seventy-two." By that time, she was actually nearly eighty years old.

Finally on May 29, 1848, Congress passed a bill and purchased the remaining Madison papers for twenty-five thousand dollars. Five thousand dollars was given to Dolley Madison immediately, and the remaining twenty thousand dollars was invested for her benefit. The proceeds from the investments were to provide her with a small income for the rest of her life.

A few days before Congress purchased James Madison's papers, they were almost destroyed when Dolley Madison's house caught fire. Mrs. Madison was in her bedroom sound asleep when one of her neighbors noticed the fire. He quickly woke Madison's servants, and her faithful butler ran upstairs to get his mistress. She would not leave

This portrait shows Dolley Madison as she looked in her later years.

until the butler promised to save her husband's papers. Later, Dolley Madison had a hearty laugh when she remembered the way she had been unceremoniously moved "from a warm bed to cold grass with her bare feet," and that her best black velvet dress had been thrown out the window for her to put on "at three o'clock in the morning!"[24]

One of Dolley Madison's last public appearances was in February 1849 at a formal reception given by President James K. Polk. Dolley Madison was one of Polk's favorites and an honored guest at the reception. She sat on a raised platform throughout the evening. Just before the reception ended, President Polk walked through the crowded rooms with Dolley Madison on his arm.

Dolley Madison's Death

In July 1849, it became apparent to Dolley Madison's friends and family that her health was beginning to fail. During her last days, she occupied her time reminiscing about the past and reading the

White House
After the fire in August 1814, the inside of the President's House was rebuilt and the outside of the house was painted white. At the time, people started calling the mansion the White House. In 1901, President Theodore Roosevelt officially authorized the title of White House for the executive mansion.

Bible. The Gospel of St. John was her favorite scripture, and while it was being read to her, she fell into a long sleep. She slept eighteen hours before her family became concerned and sent for her physician. He determined that she had suffered a stroke.

For two days, Dolley Madison remained unconscious. Occasionally, according to her niece, Mary Cutts, she would wake up when she heard her son's voice and utter the words, "My poor boy."[25] At other times she would awaken for a short time and smile, with her arms stretched out as if to embrace her many friends and family members standing nearby. Dolley Madison died on July 12, 1849, between ten and eleven o'clock in the evening.

10

EPILOGUE

On July 14, 1849, the *National Intelligencer* ran the announcement of Dolley Madison's death in an article bordered in black:

> It is with saddened hearts that we announce to our readers the decease of Mrs. Madison, Widow of James Madison, Ex-President of the United States. . . . Beloved by all who personally knew her, and universally respected, this venerable Lady closed her long and well-spent life with calm resignation.[1]

After her death, Dolley Madison's body was placed in a sarcophagus, a stone coffin, that had been sent from New York. Early in the morning on July 16, her coffin was moved across the street to

St. John's Episcopal Church, where hundreds of people filed past the altar to pay their last respects to the former First Lady. At four o'clock that afternoon, Reverend Smith Pyne conducted Dolley Madison's funeral service.

After the service, a large procession of carriages followed her coffin to the Congressional Cemetery, where Payne Todd requested that his mother's body be temporarily placed. The procession was the largest one ever seen in the city. It included family members, President James Polk and his Cabinet, the diplomatic corps, members of the Senate and the House of Representatives, judges from both the Supreme Court and district courts, military officers, the mayor and other city officials, and finally, local citizens.

In her will, Dolley Madison left her son ten thousand dollars, half of the funds that had been invested for her after the last sale of her husband's papers. The other half of the funds she left to Anna Payne, her niece and constant companion. Payne Todd felt he should have been his mother's sole heir. He forged another will, leaving everything to himself, and contested her will. He was unsuccessful and his mother's wishes prevailed.

After her aunt's death, Anna Payne found a new home with Dr. Thomas Miller and his family. Miller had been a close friend of Dolley Madison's and was delighted a few months later when Anna Payne married one of his colleagues, Dr. James Causten. Anna Payne died three years later.

Shortly after Anna Payne's death, Payne Todd died of typhoid fever in a Washington hotel. His only attendants were his two slaves. His coffin was followed by one unnamed person as it was carried through the streets to the Congressional Cemetery. The *National Intelligencer* ran a belated announcement of his death on January 27, 1852.

On February 10, 1852, Dolley Madison's coffin was transferred from the vault in the Congressional Cemetery to the privately owned vault of James Causten, Anna Payne's husband. Six years later, on January 12, 1858, family members had Dolley Madison's body moved to Virginia, where she was

Dolley Madison Collection

Dolley Madison's personal property was sold at a public auction in 1852. Her family and friends purchased most of her belongings. The majority of the items were acquired by her niece, Mary Causten, Anna Payne's daughter. After Causten's death, her son, John Kunkel, became the guardian of Dolley Madison's belongings. For over twenty years they were carefully preserved and hidden away in the attic of his home in Allentown, Pennsylvania. They were discovered after his death and purchased by the Greensboro Historical Museum.

Dolley Madison is buried next to her husband at Montpelier.

finally buried next to her husband in the Madison family cemetery at Montpelier.

For most of her life, Dolley Madison had been our nation's greatest hostess. She defined the role of First Lady for future presidents' wives and inspired them with her gracious manners and patriotism. President Martin Van Buren called her "the most brilliant hostess this country has ever known."[2] But President Zachary Taylor said it best when he declared that "she will never be forgotten because she was truly our First Lady for a half-century."[3]

CHRONOLOGY

1768—Born in Guilford County, North Carolina, on May 20.

1790—Marries John Todd, Jr., on January 7.

1792—Son John Payne Todd born on February 29.

1793—Yellow fever epidemic; Son William Temple born in September; Husband, John Todd, and son William Temple die on October 24.

1794—Introduced to Congressman James Madison in April; Marries Madison on September 15; Disowned by the Quakers for marrying outside their Society in December.

1797—Leaves Philadelphia with husband to live at Montpelier, the Madison family home, in _Virginia.

1801—James Madison appointed secretary of state by President Thomas Jefferson; Dolley Madison acts as President Jefferson's official hostess at the President's House._

1803—Louisiana Purchase; Lewis and Clark expedition.

1805—Stricken with knee infection and spends over three months in Philadelphia under doctor's care.

1809—James Madison inaugurated as the fourth president of the United States on March 4.

1812—War declared between the United States and Great Britain.

1813—James Madison inaugurated for his second term of office.

1814—British fleet lands on the coast of Maryland on June 22 and invades Washington, D.C.

1815—President Madison signs Treaty of Ghent in February, officially ending the War of 1812.

1817—James Madison ends his second term in office and returns home to Virginia.

1836—James Madison dies on June 28.

1837—Moves to Washington, D.C.; Congress purchases James Madison's notes from the Constitutional Convention.

1839—Goes back to Montpelier in an attempt to save
–1841 the plantation.

1841—Returns to Washington, D.C.

1842—Sells first half of Montpelier.

1844—Granted permanent seat in the Congressional Hall; Watches Samuel F. B. Morse send first telegraph message; Sells remainder of Montpelier.

1848—Congress purchases the remainder of James Madison's papers.

1849—Dies on July 12.

CHAPTER NOTES

Chapter 1. The British Are Coming!

1. Elizabeth L. Dean, *Dolly Madison, the Nation's Hostess* (Boston: Lothrop, Lee, & Shepard Co., 1928), p. 132.

2. Allen C. Clark, *Life and Letters of Dolly Madison* (Washington, D.C.: Press of W. F. Roberts Co., 1914), p. 164.

3. Paul Jennings, *Colored Man's Reminiscences of James Madison* (Brooklyn: George C. Beadle, 1865), p. 10.

4. Clark, p. 165.

5. Jennings, p. 11.

6. Dolley Madison, *Memoirs and Letters of Dolly Madison, Wife of James Madison, President of the United States*, ed. Lucia B. Cutts (Port Washington, N.Y.: Kennikat Press, 1886), p. 104.

7. Ethel S. Arnett, *Mrs. James Madison: The Incomparable Dolley* (Greensboro, N.C.: Piedmont Press, 1972), p. 225.

8. Ibid.

9. Ibid., pp. 227–228.

10. Ibid., p. 229.

11. Ibid.

12. Ibid., p. 231.

13. Ibid., p. 233.

14. Noel B. Gerson, *The Velvet Glove* (Nashville, Tenn.: Thomas Nelson Publishers, 1975), p. 223.

Chapter 2. Quaker Girl

1. Virginia Moore, *The Madisons: A Biography* (New York: McGraw-Hill Book Company, 1979), p. 3.

2. Katharine S. Anthony, *Dolly Madison, Her Life and Times* (Garden City, N.Y.: Doubleday, 1949), p. 10.

3. Ibid.

4. Ibid., p. 14.

5. Ibid.

6. Ibid., p. 25.

7. Allen C. Clark, *Life and Letters of Dolly Madison* (Washington, D.C.: Press of W. F. Roberts Co., 1914), p. 12.

8. Dolley Madison, *Memoirs and Letters of Dolly Madison, Wife of James Madison, President of the United States*, ed. Lucia B. Cutts (Port Washington, N.Y.: Kennikat Press, 1886), p. 10.

9. Maud W. Goodwin, *Dolly Madison* (New York: Charles Scribner's Sons, 1896), p. 33.

10. Madison, pp. 11–12.

11. Ibid., p. 13.

Chapter 3. The Great Little Madison

1. Katharine S. Anthony, *Dolly Madison, Her Life and Times* (Garden City, N.Y.: Doubleday, 1949), p. 52.

2. Virginia Moore, *The Madisons: A Biography* (New York: McGraw-Hill Book Company, 1979), p. xi.

3. Dolley Madison, *Memoirs and Letters of Dolly Madison, Wife of James Madison, President of the United States*, ed. Lucia B. Cutts (Port Washington, N.Y.: Kennikat Press, 1886), p. 14.

4. Ibid.

5. Ibid., p. 15.

6. Joy Hakim, *A History of the US: From Colonies to Country* (New York: Oxford University Press, 1993), p. 158.

7. Moore, p. 10.

8. Madison, p. 16.

9. Ibid.

10. Merill D. Peterson, ed., *James Madison: A Biography in His Own Words* (New York: Harper & Row, 1974), p. 202.

11. Moore, pp. 16–17.

12. Ibid., p. 17.

13. Noel B. Gerson, *The Velvet Glove* (Nashville, Tenn.: Thomas Nelson Publishers, 1975), p. 70.

14. Moore, p. 48.

15. Katharine S. Anthony, *Dolly Madison, Her Life and Times* (Garden City, N.Y.: Doubleday, 1949), p. 92.

16. Moore, p. 50.

17. Ibid., p. 48.

18. Ibid., pp. 49–50.

19. Gerson, p. 78.

20. Paul F. Boller, Jr., *Presidential Wives* (New York: Oxford University Press, 1988), p. 38.

21. Irving Brant, *The Fourth President: A Life of James Madison* (New York: The Bobbs-Merrill Company, Inc., 1970), p. 283.

Chapter 4. Montpelier

1. Maud W. Goodwin, *Dolly Madison* (New York: Charles Scribner's Sons, 1896), p. 75.

2. Ibid.

3. Elizabeth L. Dean, *Dolly Madison, the Nation's Hostess* (Boston: Lothrop, Lee, & Shepard Co., 1928), p. 77.

4. Virginia Moore, *The Madisons: A Biography* (New York: McGraw-Hill Book Company, 1979), p. 88.

5. Ibid.

6. Ibid., pp. 90–91.

7. Irving Brant, *The Fourth President: A Life of James Madison* (New York: The Bobbs-Merrill Company, Inc., 1970), p. 295.

8. Ibid., p. 294.

9. Noel B. Gerson, *The Velvet Glove* (Nashville, Tenn.: Thomas Nelson Publishers, 1975), p. 105

10. Moore, p. 148.

11. Dean, p. 83.

Chapter 5. Jefferson's Hostess

1. Virginia Moore, *The Madisons: A Biography* (New York: McGraw-Hill Book Company, 1979), p. 157.

2. Joy Hakim, *A History of the US: The New Nation* (New York: Oxford University Press, 1993), p. 32.

3. Fawn Brodie, *Thomas Jefferson: An Intimate History* (New York: Bantam, 1974), p. 336.

4. Elizabeth L. Dean, *Dolly Madison, the Nation's Hostess* (Boston: Lothrop, Lee, & Shepard Co., 1928), p. 94.

5. Ibid., p. 91.

6. Maud W. Goodwin, *Dolly Madison* (New York: Charles Scribner's Sons, 1896), p. 87.

7. Ibid.

8. Katharine S. Anthony, *Dolly Madison, Her Life and Times* (Garden City, N.Y.: Doubleday, 1949), p. 126.

9. Ibid., p. 127.

10. Marianne Means, *The Woman in the White House* (New York: Random House, 1963), p. 66.

11. Ibid.

12. Anthony, p. 118.

13. Moore, pp. 163–164.

14. Dean, p. 98.

15. Anthony, p. 146.

16. Dolley Madison, *Memoirs and Letters of Dolly Madison, Wife of James Madison, President of the United States*, ed. Lucia B. Cutts (Port Washington, N.Y.: Kennikat Press, 1886), p. 42.

17. Allen C. Clark, *Life and Letters of Dolly Madison* (Washington, D.C.: Press of W.F. Roberts Co., 1914), p. 77.
18. Ibid., p. 79.
19. Anthony, p. 169.
20. Ibid., p. 171.
21. Moore, p. 200.
22. Irving Brant, *The Fourth President: A Life of James Madison* (New York: The Bobbs-Merrill Company, Inc., 1970), p. 383.
23. Roger Bruns, *Jefferson* (New York: Chelsea House Publishers, 1986), p. 98.
24. Noel B. Gerson, *The Velvet Glove* (Nashville, Tenn.: Thomas Nelson Publishers, 1975), p. 177.

Chapter 6. The President's Lady
1. Virginia Moore, *The Madisons: A Biography* (New York: McGraw-Hill Book Company, 1979), p. 220.
2. Maud W. Goodwin, *Dolly Madison* (New York: Charles Scribner's Sons, 1896), p. 126.
3. Margaret Bayard Smith (Mrs. Samuel Harrison), *The First Forty Years of Washington Society*, ed. Gaillard Hunt (New York: Charles Scribner's Sons, 1906), p. 59.
4. Ibid., p. 58.
5. Ibid., p. 62.
6. Louise Durbin, *Inaugural Cavalcade* (New York: Dodd Mead & Company, 1971), p. 26.
7. Elizabeth L. Dean, *Dolly Madison, the Nation's Hostess* (Boston: Lothrop, Lee, & Shepard Co., 1928), p. 113.
8. Smith, p. 61.
9. Ibid., p. 63.
10. William Seale, *The President's House: A History* (Washington, D.C.: White House Historical Association, 1986), vol. 1, p. 128.
11. Ethel S. Arnett, *Mrs. James Madison: The Incomparable Dolley* (Greensboro, N.C.: Piedmont Press, 1972), p. 172.
12. Paul Dickson, *The Great American Ice Cream Book* (New York: Atheneum, 1978), pp. 15–24.
13. Goodwin, pp. 140–141.
14. Katharine S. Anthony, *Dolly Madison, Her Life and Times* (Garden City, N.Y.: Doubleday, 1949), p. 202.
15. Ibid.
16. Arnett, p. 186.

Chapter 7. War of 1812

1. Ethel S. Arnett, *Mrs. James Madison: The Incomparable Dolley* (Greensboro, N.C.: Piedmont Press, 1972), p. 207.

2. Katharine S. Anthony, *Dolly Madison, Her Life and Times* (Garden City, N.Y.: Doubleday, 1949), p. 210.

3. Maud W. Goodwin, *Dolly Madison* (New York: Charles Scribner's Sons, 1896), p. 151.

4. Margaret L. Coit, *The Life History of the United States, The Growing Years* (New York: Time-Life Books, 1963), vol. 3, p. 102.

5. Goodwin, p. 157.

6. Anthony, p. 212.

7. Arnett, pp. 211–212.

8. Joy Hakim, *A History of the US: The New Nation* (New York: Oxford University Press, 1993), p. 79.

9. Robert A. Rutland, *James Madison and the Search for Nationhood* (Washington, D.C.: The Library of Congress, 1981), p. 150.

10. Hakim, p. 80.

11. Arnett, p. 421.

12. Ibid.

Chapter 8. Peace

1. Katharine S. Anthony, *Dolly Madison, Her Life and Times* (Garden City, N.Y.: Doubleday, 1949), p. 238.

2. Paul Jennings, *A Colored Man's Reminiscences of James Madison* (Brooklyn: George C. Beadle, 1865), p. 15.

3. Anthony, p. 239.

4. Ibid., pp. 243–244.

5. Virginia Moore, *The Madisons: A Biography* (New York: McGraw-Hill Book Company, 1979), p. 361.

6. Anthony, p. 251.

7. Ethel S. Arnett, *Mrs. James Madison: The Incomparable Dolley* (Greensboro, N.C.: Piedmont Press, 1972), p. 199.

8. Moore, p. 360.

9. Maud W. Goodwin, *Dolly Madison* (New York: Charles Scribner's Sons, 1896), p. 192.

10. Arnett, p. 261.

Chapter 9. Later Years

1. Irving Brant, *The Fourth President: A Life of James Madison* (New York: The Bobbs-Merrill Co., Inc., 1970), p. 607.

2. Ibid.

3. Elizabeth L. Dean, *Dolly Madison, the Nation's Hostess* (Boston: Lothrop, Lee, & Shepard Co., 1928), p. 192.

4. Ibid.

5. Allen C. Clark, *Life and Letters of Dolly Madison* (Washington, D.C.: Press of W.F. Roberts Co., 1914), p. 233.

6. Margaret Bayard Smith (Mrs. Samuel Harrison), *The First Forty Years of Washington Society* (New York: Charles Scribner's Sons, 1906), p. 236.

7. Ethel S. Arnett, *Mrs. James Madison: The Incomparable Dolley* (Greensboro, N.C.: Piedmont Press, 1972), p. 300.

8. Maud W. Goodwin, *Dolly Madison* (New York: Charles Scribner's Sons, 1896), p. 240.

9. Ibid., pp. 230–231.

10. Ibid., p. 234.

11. Arnett, p. 320.

12. Brant, p. 641.

13. Paul Jennings, *A Colored Man's Reminiscences of James Madison* (Brooklyn: George C. Beadle, 1865), p. 20.

14. Ibid.

15. Ibid.

16. Virginia Moore, *The Madisons: A Biography* (New York: McGraw-Hill Book Company, 1979), p. 478.

17. Katherine S. Anthony, *Dolly Madison, Her Life and Times* (Garden City, N.Y.: Doubleday, 1949), p. 330.

18. Arnett, p. 329.

19. Ibid., p. 330.

20. Dean, p. 226.

21. Jennings, pp. 16–17.

22. Arnett, p. 353.

23. Ibid.

24. Ibid., pp. 376–377.

25. Ibid., p. 391.

Chapter 10. Epilogue

1. Elizabeth L. Dean, *Dolly Madison, the Nation's Hostess* (Boston: Lothrop, Lee, & Shepard Co., 1928), p. 241.

2. Paul F. Boller, Jr., *Presidential Wives* (New York: Oxford University Press, 1988), p. 43.

3. Ibid., p. 36.

GLOSSARY

arbor—A shady resting place in a garden, often made of rustic wood or latticework that is covered with vines.

carpet slippers—House shoes.

couple—To link together; connect.

decanter—A decorative bottle used for serving wine.

emancipation—Freedom from bondage.

fireside—A place near the fire or hearth; home.

frigate—A high-speed, medium-sized warship.

impress—To force into service.

infirmity—A body ailment or weakness, especially one brought on by old age.

levee—A formal reception.

litter—A device for carrying a sick or injured person; a stretcher.

malaria—An infectious disease transmitted by mosquitoes and characterized by cycles of chills, fever, and sweating.

mason—One who builds or works with stone or brick.

mast—A tall vertical pole that rises from the deck of a sailing vessel to support the sails and rigging.

minister—An authorized diplomatic representative of a government.

nightcap—A cloth cap worn in bed.

nullify—To cancel or repeal.

parlor—A room in a private home set apart for the

entertainment of visitors.

portico—A porch or walkway with a roof supported by columns, often leading to the entrance of a building.

profusion—Abundance.

repugnant—Disgusting or offensive.

rheumatism—A chronic disease marked by stiffness and inflammation of the joints, weakness, loss of mobility, and deformity.

sideboards—A piece of dining-room furniture having drawers and shelves for linens and tableware.

sloop—One-masted sailing vessel.

splint—A rigid device used to prevent motion of a joint.

spy glass—A small telescope.

sumptuous—Very rich, expensive, luxurious, or splendid.

Yankee—An American.

FURTHER READING

Books

Anthony, Katharine S. *Dolly Madison, Her Life and Times.* Garden City, N.Y.: Doubleday, 1949.

Arnett, Ethel S. *Mrs. James Madison: The Incomparable Dolley.* Greensboro, N.C.: Piedmont Press, 1972.

Brant, Irving. *The Fourth President: A Life of James Madison.* New York: The Bobbs-Merrill Co., Inc., 1970.

Brodie, Fawn M. *Thomas Jefferson: An Intimate Story.* New York: Bantam Books, 1974.

Fritz, Jean. *The Great Little Madison.* New York: G. P. Putnam's Sons, 1989.

Hakim, Joy. *A History of the US: From Colonies to Country.* New York: Oxford University Press, 1993.

———. *A History of the US: The New Nation.* New York: Oxford University Press, 1993.

Malone, Mary. *James Madison.* Springfield, N.J.: Enslow Publishers, Inc., 1997.

Moore, Virginia. *The Madisons: A Biography.* New York: McGraw-Hill Book Company, 1979.

Old, Wendie C. *Thomas Jefferson.* Springfield, N.J.: Enslow Publishers, Inc., 1997.

Internet

"Dolley Payne Todd Madison." *The First Ladies of the United States of America.* n.d.<http://www.whitehouse.gov/WH/glimpse/firstladies/html/dm4-plain.html>(May 8, 1998).

The James Madison Museum. February 14, 1997. <http://www.gemlink.com/~jmmuseum/home2.htm> (July 1, 1998).

Skemp, Sheila L. "The American Presidency." *Grolier Online.* 1996.<http://www.grolier.com/presidents/aae/first/04pw.html>(May 8, 1998).

"Todd House." *UShistory.org.* n.d. <http://www.libertynet.org/iha/tour/_todd.html>(May 8, 1998).

INDEX

A

Adams, Abigail, 37, 51
Adams, John, 37, 39, 40, 41,
    45, 49, 51, 54

B

Burr, Aaron, 25, 39, 49, 52,
    62

C

Cutts, Anna Payne (sister),
    16, 24, 29, 32, 34, 53, 58,
    60, 63, 70, 77, 95, 96–97,
    102

D

Dandridge, Dorothea, 15

H

Hamilton, Alexander, 36, 44,
    62, 63
Henry, Patrick, 15, 16, 18,
    47–48

J

Jefferson, Thomas, 22, 34–35,
    36, 39, 43, 44, 46, 47, 49,
    50, 52, 53, 54, 55, 60, 62,
    63, 65, 66, 67, 68, 69, 70,
    74, 83, 91, 98
Jennings, Paul, 8, 89, 90, 98,
    106

L

Lee, Elizabeth Collins, 25, 27,
    31

M

Madison, Dolley Payne Todd,
    14, 16, 24, 25, 27, 28,
33–34, 40, 42, 43, 44–45,
47, 49, 55, 58, 63–64, 68,
69, 71, 74, 77, 80, 82, 89,
91, 96, 98, 100, 101–102,
104–105, 106, 107, 109,
112, 113, 115
    birth, 15
    childhood, 17
    children, 22, 23, 24, 27,
        28, 29, 32, 33, 34,
        45, 53, 87, 92, 97,
        104, 112, 113
    death, 109–110, 111
    education, 17
    fashion, 35–36, 56, 58,
        69, 93
    marriages, 20, 21, 29,
        30–32
    receptions and parties,
        37, 56, 62, 64–65,
        69, 73–74, 75–76,
        92–93, 95
    saving presidential
        papers, 8, 8, 13
Madison, James (husband),
    7–8, 10, 13, 25, 27–28, 29,
    30, 31, 32, 33, 34, 36, 38,
    39, 40, 42–43, 44–45, 46,
    47, 48, 49, 52–53, 55, 56,
    60, 63, 64, 67, 68, 69, 70,
    73–74, 75, 78, 82, 84, 87,
    90, 91, 92, 95, 97, 98–99,
    107, 111
Madison, Nelly, 35, 41, 96
Montpelier, 30, 34, 38, 39,
    41, 42, 44, 45, 47, 52, 53,
    91, 94, 95, 96, 97, 100,
    101, 102, 105, 115

O

Octagon House, 89, 91

P

Payne, Isaac (brother), 16, 35
Payne, John (brother), 16, 101
Payne, John (father), 14, 15, 16–17, 18, 20, 21, 25
Payne, Mary (sister), 16, 47
Payne, Mary Coles (mother), 14, 15, 16–17, 18, 20, 21, 23, 24, 29
Payne, Walter (brother), 15, 35
Payne, William (brother), 15, 35
Philadelphia, Pennsylvania, 18, 22, 23, 24, 27, 28, 33, 34, 35, 40, 41, 44, 45, 50, 63, 64, 97
President's House, 8, 10, 13, 51, 52, 53, 54, 56, 61, 71, 73, 74, 76, 89, 102, 109

Q

Quakers, 14, 15, 16, 17, 18, 20, 21, 25, 27, 29, 31, 33, 34, 51, 73. *See also* Society of Friends.

S

Scotchtown plantation, 15, 16
Society of Friends, 16, 30. *See also* Quakers.
Stuart, Gilbert, 58

T

Todd, John (husband), 20–21, 22, 25
Todd, John Payne (son), 22, 23, 24, 27, 28, 29, 32, 33, 34, 43, 45, 53, 87, 92, 97, 104, 112, 113
Todd, Lucy Payne Washington (sister), 16, 24, 28, 29, 47, 76, 102
Todd, William Temple (son), 22, 23

W

War of 1812, 7–8, 9–12, 77–80, 82–84, 86–87, 88, 89, 91, 93
Washington, D.C., 7, 10, 11, 12, 13, 50, 51, 52, 53, 54, 56, 58, 60, 62, 63, 64, 68, 74, 76, 83, 84, 87, 89, 91, 93, 94, 95, 100, 102, 104, 106, 113
Washington, George, 9, 13, 24, 28, 36, 38, 39, 40–41, 47, 49, 50, 51, 74
Washington, Martha, 28–29, 49